Perpetuating the *Masorah*

Halakhic, Ethical, and Experiential Dimensions

OU PRESS

מגיד
MAGGID

Rabbi Professor Yitzhak Twersky,
The Talner Rebbe

Perpetuating the Masorah

Halakhic, Ethical, and Experiential Dimensions

Essays in Memory of Rabbi Joseph B. Soloveitchik

EDITED BY
Carmi Horowitz
and
David Shapiro

OU Press
Maggid Books

Perpetuating the Masorah
Halakhic, Ethical, and Experiential Dimensions

First Maggid Edition, 2023

Maggid Books
An imprint of Koren Publishers Jerusalem Ltd.

POB 8531, New Milford, CT 06776-8531, USA
& POB 4044, Jerusalem 9104001, Israel
www.korenpub.com

OU Press
an imprint of the Orthodox Union
40 Rector St
New York, NY 10006
www.oupress.org

The publication of this book was made possible through the generous support of *The Jewish Book Trust.*

ISBN 978-1-59264-604-3, *hardcover*

A CIP catalogue record for this title is available from the British Library

Printed and bound in Turkey

In memory of

Rabbi Dr. Yitzhak Asher (Isadore) Twersky זצ״ל

Those who had the zekhut of interacting with
him could not help but be awed
by the moral force of his personal example, his towering intellect,
and his personification of "vehalakhta bidrakhav."
These memories fortify and inspire me almost
daily, twenty-five years later.

Donny and Shana Feldman and family

לֹא בָרוּחַ ה׳; וְאַחַר הָרוּחַ רַעַשׁ, לֹא בָרַעַשׁ ה׳.
וְאַחַר הָרַעַשׁ אֵשׁ, לֹא בָאֵשׁ ה׳; וְאַחַר הָאֵשׁ קוֹל דְּמָמָה דַקָּה.
(מלכים א׳ יט, יא–יב)

In memory of our beloved Rebbe

Rabbi Yitzhak Asher Twersky זצ״ל

Nahum and Rina Felman and family

In grateful appreciation of

מורנו ורבנו

Rabbi Yitzhak Twersky זצ״ל

teacher, friend, spiritual guide, moral exemplar.

Steve and Sybil Levisohn

וְתֵן בְּלִבֵּנוּ בִּינָה לְהָבִין וּלְהַשְׂכִּיל לִשְׁמֹעַ לִלְמֹד וּלְלַמֵּד לִשְׁמֹר וְלַעֲשׂוֹת וּלְקַיֵּם אֶת כָּל דִּבְרֵי תַלְמוּד תּוֹרָתֶךָ בְּאַהֲבָה.

In memory and appreciation of our beloved Rebbe,

Rabbi Yitzhak Twersky זצ״ל

who was and remains a role model for us in the way of serving Hashem with both our hearts and minds.

Albert and Batsheva Ruback and family

In honor of my beloved cousin a"h
a person of giant intellect, moral integrity,
and personal family commitment,
who integrated philosophy, Halakhah, and Ḥasidut

Nahum Twersky

In Loving Memory of Our Parents

Abraham and Sylvia Wintman

אברהם צבי בן יצחק חיים
שרה בלומא בת קלמן מרדכי הכהן

Our parents' lives together devoted to family, community, and Klal Yisrael, and the especially close relationship our parents maintained with the Rav, have been a wellspring of inspiration to our entire family.

Kenny Wintman and Sandy Welkes

Contents

Preface

The first four essays in this book were originally delivered orally from 1994 to 1996 by Rabbi Professor Yitzhak Twersky, the Talner Rebbe, in memory of his father-in-law Rabbi Joseph B. Soloveitchik.[1] The last essay of the book was written by R. Twersky and published in *Tradition: A Journal of Orthodox Jewish Thought* in a special memorial issue dedicated to the Rov (vol. 30, no. 4, Summer 1996) and was newly edited for this volume.

The recordings of the first four chapters of the book were transcribed by Yehuda Galinsky. Chapter 4 was then edited by Carmi Horowitz and published in the *Torah U-Madda Journal,* vol. 8 (1998–1999) under the editorship of Jacob J. Schacter. In preparing this volume, the

1. Most of the original oral *shiurim* were delivered close to the Rov's *yahrzeit,* which is 18 Nissan. They do not appear in this volume in their original chronological order but rather in thematic sequence.

    Chapter 1, "Raise Up Many Disciples," was delivered on April 5, 1994 at Maimonides School.

    Chapter 2, "From God's Torah to the Scholar's Torah," was delivered on April 14, 1996 at Maimonides School.

    Chapter 3, "The Sages and Their Students," was delivered on June 14, 1994 at a Convention of the Rabbinical Council of America, where most of the attendees were former students of the Rov.

    Chapter 4, "Make a Fence Around the Torah," was delivered on April 23, 1995 at Maimonides School.

transcriptions of these four chapters were reviewed by Menachem Jacobowitz and edited by Carmi Horowitz and David Shapiro. In some cases, insertions were made from R. Twersky's own notes for the *shiurim*. In translating the spoken word into the written medium, rhetorical repetitions and similar aspects of the oral delivery were eliminated, although the editors tried to preserve to the best of their ability R. Twersky's voice.

All five chapters contained many Hebrew sources, only some of which were translated or paraphrased by R. Twersky. When R. Twersky translated, he would at times interpolate comments while translating; the editors preserved those interpolations in parentheses and italics when presenting his translation. In order to make this volume accessible to English readers, all Hebrew sources that were not translated orally were translated by the editors in the body of the text, and the original Hebrew was placed in footnotes. When translating, the editors consulted existing standard translations, but modified them when appropriate.

The footnotes in these articles serve several purposes in addition to presenting the Hebrew texts. Full documentation for all sources is provided. At times R. Twersky referred to ideas or texts in an aside, and in order not to break the flow of the *shiur* we relegated those to footnotes. The footnotes also contain cross-references added by the editors to other chapters in the book and to some of R. Twersky's other writings. Occasionally the editors felt the need to clarify in order to enhance the reader's understanding; brackets were used to indicate editorial insertions. In chapter 5, the original published text contained untranslated Hebrew sources. In this volume we have translated all of the Hebrew in the text and have put the original Hebrew in footnotes. In addition, R. Twersky had provided his own footnotes to his essay in *Tradition*. The footnotes of chapter 5 thus contain the original Hebrew texts of the chapter as well as R. Twersky's own footnotes.

Shortly before R. Twersky passed away on 11 Tishrei 5758, one of the editors (C.H.) discussed with him the publication of these *shiurim* and was urged to give them priority. Indeed, as mentioned, one of the *shiurim* was published shortly after his passing, but only recently was progress made in editing the others.

The other editor (D.S.) is continuing to prepare R. Twersky's *divrei Torah* for publication. *Torah of the Mind, Torah of the Heart: Divrei*

Torah of the Talner Rebbe – Bereishis, Shemos, edited by David Shapiro (Urim, 2020), will soon be followed by the volume on Vayikra through Devarim, and the publication of other *shiurei Torah* by R. Twersky is planned.

All translations from the Rambam's *Mishneh Torah, Sefer Hamadda* were taken from a new translation by Bernard Septimus (a student and colleague of R. Twersky at Harvard University), to be published by Yale University Press. We thank him as well for his help in cutting a number of Gordian knots for us. We thank Ora Wiskind for her careful editing of the introduction to this book, and we thank Jeffery Saks, editor of *Tradition,* for permission to reprint R. Twersky's appreciation of the Rov (chapter 5).

We want to express our thanks and gratitude to Matthew Miller, publisher at Koren Publishers Jerusalem and its imprint Maggid Books, to Rabbi Reuven Ziegler for his welcoming of this volume to Koren, and to the editors Ita Olesker, Debbie Ismailoff, and Efrat Gross, who provided us with expert editorial advice both stylistic and substantive. Thanks, too, to indexers Marc Sherman and Nachum Goldstein. OU Press was generous in accepting this book under their aegis as well, and we thank Rabbi Menachem Genack and Rabbi Simon Posner for their help and support.

We feel privileged to be able to present these *shiurim* to the wider public.

Carmi Horowitz
David Shapiro
Jerusalem
February 2023/ Shevat 5783

Introduction

Perpetuating the Masorah is an unusual document in the history of religious-spiritual literature. It is a collection of essays on aggadic, halakhic, ethical, and spiritual themes by Rabbi Professor Yitzhak (Isadore) Twersky (1930–1997)[1] dedicated to the memory of his father-in-law, Rabbi Joseph B. Soloveitchik. Prof. Twersky, a world-famous, world-class academic, was the Nathan Littauer Professor of Hebrew Literature and Philosophy at Harvard University, who founded and headed the university's Center for Jewish Studies. He was considered one of the outstanding Maimonidean scholars of his time and a master of medieval Jewish intellectual history with a specialty in the relationship between Halakhah and Jewish spirituality. His books and his articles became classics in his

1. For a detailed account of his life and his scholarly contributions see, Carmi Horowitz, "Halakha and History, Intellectualism and Spirituality: Prof. Isadore (Yitzhak) Twersky's Academic-Religious Profile," in Meir Soloveichik, Stuart Halpern, Shlomo Zuckier, eds., *Torah and Western Thought: Intellectual Portraits of Orthodoxy and Modernity* (Straus Center for Torah and Western Thought and Maggid Books, 2015), 249–280. An expanded Hebrew version of this article appeared in Yitzhak (Isadore) Twersky, *Kema'ayan Hamitgaber: Law and Spirit in Medieval Jewish Thought* (Heb.), edited by Carmi Horowitz (The Zalman Shazar Center, 2020), 29–58. An earlier biographical article, idem, "Professor Yitzchak Twersky – The Talner Rebbe *z"l*: A Brief Biography" appeared in the *Torah U-Madda Journal*, vol. 8, 1998–1999, 41–58.

lifetime, and they continue to be studied and quoted. His magnum opus, *Introduction to the Code of Maimonides (Mishneh Torah)*, is a brilliant and innovative study of Maimonides' Code of Law. His writing is effervescent, teeming with insights and new understandings of Maimonides, in both the text of the book and the incredibly rich footnotes, which gesture to myriad potential new directions in the study of Maimonidean thought. In addition, a volume of thirty-one of his academic articles was recently published in Hebrew, entitled *Kema'ayan Hamitgaber*.[2] Those collected essays showcase the breadth and depth of his thought, including new studies on central themes in Maimonidean thought; the complementary relationship between Halakhah and meta-halakhic disciplines, such as philosophy, Kabbalah, works on ethics and Ḥasidism, that provided the spiritual-intellectual underpinning of Halakhah; studies of major halakhic figures, and of commentators to the Bible and to *aggadot Ḥazal*; and incisive essays on some important contemporary themes.

Simultaneous with his career at Harvard University, R. Twersky succeeded his father, R. Meshulem Zusha Twersky, as the ḥasidic head of Beit Hamidrash Beit David in Brookline, and served there as the Talner Rebbe. There he prayed, taught Torah, and guided the congregants. R. Twersky was deeply committed to his role as the Rebbe, and while he dispensed with some of the externalities of ḥasidic garb, he saw himself as a link in the chain of ḥasidic tradition. He was as punctilious in preserving ḥasidic customs as he was in his halakhic observance, and was a compassionate leader who cared for and took close interest in his congregants. And just as he praised his father-in-law for his bountiful *ḥesed*, his own *ḥesed* was extensive and sensitive, yet covert and concealed.

The essays in this volume reveal one more facet of R. Twersky's legacy, and that is the profound impact that his father-in-law the Rov, R. Joseph B. Soloveitchik, had upon him. R. Twersky writes in the introduction to his book on Maimonides how he "repeatedly benefitted from his [father-in-law's] immense and genuinely effervescent learning... [he] has given me so much over the years that it would be folly to assume that formal acknowledgement would be fully expressive." The first four

2. See previous note. Of the thirty-one, seventeen were translated into Hebrew from the original English; the other fourteen were originally written in Hebrew.

chapters in this volume were *shiurim* by R. Twersky in tribute to the Rov; they were not intended to be a *hesped*. However, the "presence" of the Rov is felt in all of them, either explicitly or implicitly. The themes that are developed were important to both of them, and in *Perpetuating the Masorah* R. Twersky is also perpetuating the legacy of the Rov. The chapters of this volume offer insight into the Rov's influence on him, notwithstanding his own independent and original thinking and writing.

R. Prof. Twersky's academic writing was as profound as it was all-encompassing. Although he ostensibly dealt with historical and conceptual issues in the detached mode of a Harvard scholar, the discerning reader can sense an undercurrent of identification, of passion, of an almost experiential fusion with the topics and personalities that concerned him.

That the (understated) ardor and passion were truly there could be corroborated by the personal experience of davening at the Talner *beit midrash*, by meeting the Talner Rebbe and hearing him deliver a classic *shiur* in Talmud, short and incisive *divrei Torah* at *seudah shelishit* at the Talner shul,[3] and at times longer, fully developed *shiurim*, all of which were blended with original, creative understanding of Torah verses, of talmudic discussions, and of aggadic homilies and narratives. The readers of the essays in this volume will get a glimpse of all of the above. These are not intellectually detached scholarly essays but rather edited transcriptions of his carefully crafted oral *shiurim*. Commitment to the *masorah*, the passion and love of Torah, the excitement of understanding *penimiyut hatorah* – the inner spirituality of Torah – all flow from the words and from between the words of these essays.

The essays in this volume all relate to the content of the *masorah*, the tradition of the Written and Oral Law revealed at Sinai, and its preservation and transmission throughout the generations. Some of the topics are: the teaching of Torah and its goals; how one becomes a Torah scholar; the prerogatives of Torah scholars as well as their responsibilities and obligations; the ways in which Torah should be taught; the qualities of teachers of Torah as well as of students of Torah; and,

3. See Harav Yitzhak (Isadore) Twersky, *Torah of the Mind, Torah of the Heart: Divrei Torah of the Talner Rebbe – Bereishis, Shemos*, ed. David Shapiro (Urim, 2020).

finally, the uniqueness of Jewish tradition. The *masorah* emphasizes the centrality of law, which included its observance as well as the heavy intellectual demands of its study, while simultaneously giving a place of preeminence to religious spirituality, and to moral and ethical living. This fusion of law and spirituality was a central focus in Prof. Twersky's scholarly writings, but for him the topic was not solely academic. It lay at the very heart of his own religious consciousness, his own spiritual commitment to a life of *kedushah,* holiness. It was a cherished and honored feature of the spiritual legacies he had inherited: the ḥasidic tradition he received from his father, and the intellectual-spiritual heritage he received from his father-in-law.

HALAKHAH AND AGGADAH, LAW AND SPIRITUALITY

One of R. Twersky's central goals in these collected essays is to demonstrate the interconnectedness of Halakhah and Aggadah. He stated that goal explicitly in the opening of the oral version of chapter 1: "The decision I reached... was to combine the two areas of Halakhah and Aggadah, starting with a halakhah found at the beginning of *Pirkei Avot, ha'amidu talmidim harbeh,* 'raise up many disciples.'" Take note that R. Twersky defines that maxim as "Halakhah," although generally the statements of *Ḥazal* in *Pirkei Avot* are considered aggadic. This puts into sharp relief R. Twersky's goal of perceiving Halakhah and Aggadah as two complementary realms.

The significance of the close relationship between Halakhah and Aggadah in R. Twersky's thinking goes beyond the connections between two genres of rabbinic literature. It is part and parcel of his understanding of the relationship between law and spirituality. The cluster of concepts "spirituality," "intellectual-spiritual," "religious," "moral," and "ethical" are in fact a leitmotif in the chapters of this book, evoking fundamental ideas and ideals of his thought. Their importance and centrality concerned him not only in these *shiurim,* but in his scholarly writings as well.

In his academic writings, Prof. Twersky describes Halakhah as "the indispensable manifestation and prescribed concretization of an underlying and overriding spiritual essence, a volatile, magnetic and incompressible religious force designated as Judaism." According to this view, one cannot separate the legal-halakhic norms, which are the external manifestation of Judaism, from the "internal sensibility and spirituality" that is at its core. Halakhah "is a means for the actualization and celebration of ethical norms, historical experiences and theological postulates." It is accompanied by a "spiritualizing speculative quest, in philosophic, mystical or pietistic terms" which ensures "that action is reflective and deliberate, that the religious performance is both an expression of as well as stimulus to experience, deep and rich, full and fresh."[4] The theme of Halakhah and spirituality reverberates throughout the generations, and Prof. Twersky pays close attention to its dynamics in the chapters of the book.

R. Twersky's modes of teaching and writing varied, as did his style and goals. His scholarly works were written within the orbit of his position as professor at Harvard University, and his readers were students, professors, and scholars of Jewish studies. R. Twersky strictly adhered to the objective rigor required of such writing, and his published writings were all intended for an academic audience. Yet his Torah teaching, his *divrei Torah*, his *shiurim*, delivered in the mode of classic Torah study, were also of great importance to him. As mentioned in the Preface, he encouraged us to publish these *shiurim*. Despite the difference in mode, for him there was no dissonance between his academic writing and his Torah teaching. In that context, the late Prof. Ezra Fleisher eloquently formulated his perception of his close friend Yitzhak Twersky's harmonious persona. The following excerpt is from a *hesped* for R. Twersky at a *shloshim* in his memory held at the Israel Academy for Sciences.

> Yitzhak Twersky was a man of inner harmony, a great believer in the holistic nature of the human spirit and the fundamental unity of existence. He was at peace with his contradictions and amused by (what seemed to our commonplace vision to be) the paradoxes that seemed to define his being. Whoever came in contact with him found all this puzzling; he himself never ceased to be puzzled by their puzzlement. Indeed, at lofty heights apparent opposites reveal their true nature as varied manifestations

4. The phrases in quotation marks in this paragraph are taken from Isadore Twersky, "Religion and Law," in *Studies in Jewish Law and Philosophy* (Ktav, 1982), 69–70.

> of a single wondrous unity, while only the small-minded and myopic are still pained by their dissonance. Those heights were Yitzhak Twersky's natural, chosen vantage point. He considered the objects of his scholarly research, each in its particularity, from that vantage point and, with generous regard, perceived our nation's history in all its complexity. His eyes were too pure to see contradictions. The harmonious wholeness of his own refined spirit enabled him to discern the same in our history, and to understand the mystery of its hidden unity.[5]

Thus, while the student and the reader may still be struck by the changes in register between R. Twersky's academic mode and his mode as a teacher of Torah, he himself glided easily between them.

OVERVIEW OF *PERPETUATING THE MASORAH*

Chapter 1: Raise Up Many Disciples

The first chapter focuses on a maxim in the opening mishnah of *Pirkei Avot,* "raise up many disciples." As an introduction to *Pirkei Avot,* R. Twersky discusses two elements of Jewish ethics: the first is the inseparability of the ethical norm from the act of faith, and the negation of a self-sustaining secular ethic; the second is how ethical and moral principles have no rigid boundaries and are dependent upon each individual's knowledge, sensitivity, and determination.

"Raise up many disciples" is a principle crucial for the preservation and perpetuation of the *masorah,* for it sets the context of ensuring that disciples will continue the *masorah.* There are two traditions in the history of teaching Torah: one restrictive and elitist, the other expansive and egalitarian. The halakhic ramifications of this principle concern whether Torah should be taught to all without any supervisory control, or whether strict limits on who enters the classroom may be set. Halakhic decisors in codes and responsa deal with the issue.

5. Ezra Fleisher, "*Hesped,*" in *A Memorial for Yitzhak Twersky: Addresses on the Occasion of Thirty Days After His Passing* [Hebrew] (The Israel Academy for the Sciences, 1997), 8.

R. Twersky elucidates the qualities of the ideal teacher of Torah and, as is true of many ethical and moral principles, these qualities are of an open-ended nature. He notes three qualities: *ḥesed,* kindness, the willingness to share wisdom with others; *tzniut,* humility, which enables the teacher to communicate effectively with all who are eager to acquire learning; and the need to instill self-confidence and independence in students, giving them the ability to develop intellectually and spiritually.

The teaching of Torah with comprehensiveness, precision, and clarity is crucial for the preservation of the *masorah,* and hence an important facet of "raise up many disciples." Comprehensiveness is realized not only through intellectual communication but also by imparting the *nishmat hatorah,* the inner essence of Torah, the excitement and exhilaration of the encounter with God that accompanied and continues to accompany the study of Torah and the performance of mitzvot.

Chapter 2: From God's Torah to the Scholar's Torah

The preservation of the *masorah* is guaranteed by scholars who commit themselves to the study of the Torah. In this chapter R. Twersky presents a rabbinic homily on a verse in Tehillim that describes the process a student of Torah must undergo in order to acquire deep and extensive knowledge of Torah and transform God's Torah into *Torah dilei,* his own Torah. A series of halakhot consequent to the homily follow; they deal with the status and privileges of one who acquires knowledge of Torah, now considered a scholar, as well as the responsibilities and obligations of that scholar.

The obligations of the Torah scholar are all rooted in spiritual and intellectual integrity and demand a life of commitment to the transmission of Torah to all students, with special emphasis on the very young. Among those responsibilities are sustaining high ethical and intellectual standards, and possessing impeccable scruples in one's relationship with other scholars. All of this while internalizing moral and ethical integrity and humility as guiding principles in all of one's activities.

Chapter 3: The Sages and Their Students

This chapter continues the theme of the perpetuation of the *masorah* through an explication of discipleship and its implications. R. Twersky addresses the questions: Who is a genuine student of a *ḥakham*? What are the qualities of mind and soul that a student must possess to be considered a student of the wise? Becoming a *talmid* requires attentiveness to the teacher's instruction and to his behavior. True discipleship is defined as correctly understanding the core teachings of a *talmid ḥakham,* not blurring the uniqueness of his Torah by utilizing inappropriate categories and concepts foreign to Torah.

A detailed discussion carefully defines the nature of *shimush talmidei ḥakhamim,* serving and aiding scholars, as well as its halakhot, extending its responsibilities beyond the concrete and material help a student may give. *Shimush ḥakhamim* includes both learning an oral tradition and acquiring wisdom by observing scholars. The inward, experiential fulfillment of the mitzvah of *shimush* is to be in the company of Torah scholars – to see the wise as they are, in order to learn from their actions.

The teacher's responsibility toward his students is not only to transmit knowledge. He must be a paragon of ethical behavior, and thereby convey those values to others. He must also share the emotional and experiential components of his religious commitment, and project his own spiritual yearning. In this multifaceted pedagogic approach, he touches his students with his faith and enthusiasm.

Chapter 4: Make a Fence Around the Torah

The perpetuation of the *masorah* is realized not only in the qualities and attributes of the transmission, but in the way that the *masorah* is understood, absorbed, and practiced, and particularly in the way in which the *masorah* inspires, excites, indeed kindles a flame. This chapter is devoted to these aspects of preserving the *masorah.*

At first glance, the notion of "making a fence around the Torah" does not make the *masorah* seem particularly inspiring; *seyag,* a fence, ostensibly guards, protects, and prevents. Yet R. Twersky insightfully shows that *seyag* can be understood not only as restrictive, but as expansive and innovative as well. One example is the concept of *seyag* as leading to the enhancement of the Shabbat by converting it from a day of rest, a day of prohibited work, to a day of the positively experienced holiness. In a second example, he shows how the concept of *seyag* when applied to speech enhances the structure, the effectiveness, and the impact of speech.

R. Twersky goes on to show how *seyag* must be guided by the overarching principles or super-categories of Halakhah, concepts that are not mitzvot in and of themselves but rather shape or sculpt all mitzvot. Examples of those principles are *kedushah* – sanctity, and *temimut* – the joining of the intellect with the Torah. The mitzvah of *vehalakhta bidrakhav*, walking in His ways, functions in many ways as a super-category – it is a principle that triggers individuality, spirituality, and creativity. The goal is the development of religious yearning and sensitivity, and mindfulness of the mitzvot of experience, emotion, love, attitude, and perception. This enables a development of *penimiyut* – inwardness, which should be made an integral part of the religious experience of Modern Orthodoxy.

Chapter 5: The Rov

The last essay of the book was originally written by R. Twersky and published in a memorial issue of *Tradition* dedicated to the memory of the Rov, his father-in-law, R. Joseph B. Soloveitchik. It is an appreciation of the Rov, though its soaring poetic beauty perhaps warrants the term "an ode to the Rov." The picture that emerges of the Rov is that of the *ḥakham hamasorah*, the sage of tradition, par excellence.

As a halakhic scholar, his knowledge in all Torah disciplines was all-encompassing; this erudition, coupled with his creativity, powers of analysis and interpretation, insight and intuition, eloquence and charisma, gave him the extraordinary ability to communicate ideas and insights, and thus to become a trusted, thoughtful transmitter of the *masorah*. His method of teaching, the use of abstract conceptualizations of halakhic sources which sought to identify and analyze the concept that undergirds the many apparently disparate facts, was original and profound, intellectually exciting and religiously uplifting.

The other major aspect of his teaching was his unceasing, inspired preoccupation with *penimiyut hatorah* or *nishmat hatorah,* the inner spirituality of Torah. For this the Rov drew extensively on the entire range of traditional Jewish thought, to which he added insights drawn from his sovereign mastery of the Western philosophical tradition – concepts and categories that he used critically and constructively in analyzing and clarifying aspects of the *masorah*.

As one of the great *ḥakhmei hamasorah* of his time, he devoted endless energies serving as a religious and educational leader during a critical period in Jewish history, setting up and supporting educational institutions for children, serving as a communal rabbi who manifested great *ḥesed*, and assuming national leadership roles as well.

This portrait that R. Twersky paints places the Rov among the great *ḥakhmei hamasorah* of the Jewish people.

העמידו תלמידים הרבה

Chapter 1

Raise Up Many Disciples

PIRKEI AVOT: OPEN-ENDED ETHICAL PERFECTION[1]

The mishnah at the beginning of *Pirkei Avot*, which starts with *Moshe kibbel Torah misinai*, Moshe received the Torah at Sinai, elicited a very puzzling comment from R. Ovadiah Bartenura. He addressed in a very compressed form the crucial question of why the chain of tradition was chosen to introduce *Pirkei Avot* rather than being placed at the beginning of the Talmud, before Berakhot, or at the end.

1. [Rabbi Twersky opened this *shiur* with the following tribute to the Rov:

   The themes of the *shiur*, which from the vantage point of Torah study stand on their own, are automatically, without any eulogistic elaboration or *ad hominem* amplification, a tribute to the Rov. His learning underlies everything that we study and analyze, and his personal piety, benevolence, and humility illustrate in the noblest and loftiest way the principles and precepts of Judaism. To the extent that all of us here understand, appropriate, and internalize the Rov's Torah, and honestly assimilate his philosophical and ethical insights – to that extent we may proclaim that the Rov is with us, for he is among the main pillars of our eternal *masorah* community.]

> This tractate is unlike all the other tractates of the Mishnah in that it is not founded upon, it does not relate to the elaboration of a single mitzvah but is rather made up entirely of *mussarim* and *middot,* ethical statements and moral programmatic insights. Gentile scholars also wrote works of ethics (*for there is a universal literature of ethics that goes back to Aristotle and his work* The Ethics), however, these works were humanly contrived, *badu milibam,* and they deal with how man should conduct himself in relation to his fellow man. Therefore, this tractate was chosen to introduce our chain of tradition, to teach us that the *mussarim* and *middot,* moral principles and ethical virtues, in *Pirkei Avot* were not invented, they were not humanly contrived, but they were also received at Sinai.[2]

The assertion that moral principles and ethical virtues found in this tractate are not based on any mitzvah is extremely puzzling and is almost indefensible if taken literally. Anyone would almost unreflectively ask: What about the mitzvah of *vehalakhta bidrakhav,* "and you shall walk in His ways,"[3] which according to the Rambam is one of the 613 mitzvot, and by the time of the Bartenura was universally acknowledged and listed in that enumeration? Furthermore, the Gemara in Shabbat understands the verse in the *Shirah,* the Song of the Sea, *zeh Keli ve'anvehu*[4] not in the literal sense of "this is my God, I will glorify Him," but in the following manner: "Abba Sha'ul says: 'this is my God and I should be like Him, *hevei domeh lo* – as He is gracious and merciful, so you be gracious and merciful."[5]

---

2. אומר אני: לפי שמסכת זו אינה מיוסדת על פירוש מצוה ממצות התורה כשאר מסכתות שבמשנה, אלא כולה מוסרים ומדות, וחכמי אומות העולם גם כן חִברו ספרים כמו שבדו מלבם בדרכי המוסר – כיצד יתנהג אדם עם חֲברו – לפיכך התחיל התנא במסכת זו "משה קבל תורה מסיני", לומר לך שהמידות והמוסרים שבזו המסכת לא בדו אותם חכמי המשנה מלבם, אלא אף אלו מסיני (**ברטנורא**, אבות א, א).

3. Devarim 28:9.

4. Shemot 15:2.

5. אבא שאול אומר ואנוהו – הוי דומה לו, מה הוא חנון ורחום אף אתה היה חנון ורחום (שבת קלג ,ב).

The question arises then, how can the Bartenura say that this tractate, which consists entirely of moral principles and ethical virtues – and he emphasize twice that it consists of moral principles and ethical virtues – how can he say that it does not relate to the elaboration of a single mitzvah, as do the other tractates of the Mishnah? Understanding these words of the Bartenura shall be our main concern.

Beforehand, however, we must take note of his emphasis on a traditional Jewish perspective on ethics; it is a very repercussive view with far-reaching implications. He says that morality must be anchored in religious axiology. Without religious values and norms, morality will erode and collapse, will not endure, and will not resist distortion. That is why the Bartenura talks of the distinction between *mussarim* and *middot,* moral principles and ethical virtues, found in Avot as opposed to *mussarim* and *middot* found in the universal literature on ethics. The latter are humanly contrived, *shebadu milibam,* a result of human imagination and speculation. The Bartenura very forcefully underscores the difference between humanly contrived mores and the theologically based mores of Avot.[6] Actually, the Gemara illustrates this in its own exegetical, homiletical idiom that needs to be understood. The Gemara, which is quite striking, says:

> The great Ulah presented the following homily, or interpretation, at the doorstep of the house of R. Yehudah Hanasi (*note the very dramatic and public nature of the presentation*). What is the meaning of the verse "All the kings of the earth will acknowledge You because they heard the words of Your mouth"? Ulah elaborated: The verse in Tehillim does not say that they heard the *word,* the *saying* of your mouth, *in the singular,* but the *words* (*with emphasis on the plural*). When the Holy One, blessed be He, began the Ten Commandments and said *Anokhi Hashem Elokekha,* I am the Lord your God, the nations of the world (*these same nations whom the Bartenura mentions as producing humanly contrived works on ethics*) said: God is talking about His own glory; it is an act of self-glorification. (*That was the reaction of the nations of the world,*

6. See *Torah of the Mind* (p. 3, n. 3), 149–150, where this theme is also addressed.

> *when they heard the beginning of the Ten Commandments.)* When, however, he said "Honor your father and mother," they reconsidered, and acknowledged the first commandments.[7]

What is the meaning of this? What did the *ḥakhmei umot ha'olam,* the wise men of the world, think to start with? What caused them to change their mind? And finally, what happened as a result of this change?

Initially they said, *kevod atzmo Hu doresh,* He is promoting His own glory, which means that they felt that God is not concerned with social ethics, with how man gets along with his fellow man, or woman with her fellow woman, in a universal sense. Rather His interest is confined only to Himself, to abstract, self-contained, theological axioms divorced from moral practical consequences and applications. That was their reaction when they heard the first two commandments, which are theological, which affirm the existence of God and the repudiation of any idolatrous association. When, however, they heard the fifth commandment, "Honor your father and mother," they then *ḥazru vehodu lema'amarot harishonot,* they acknowledged the first commandments. It does not say that they realized that God is concerned not only with theological ethics but with social ethics as well. What the Gemara says is that they realized that without God there would be no fifth commandment to honor your father and mother. One cannot implement it properly, fully, without this religious base. There is no self-sustaining secular ethic. The wise men of the world acknowledged the inseparability of the ethical norm from the act of faith.

What I have suggested here is somewhat different from Rashi's interpretation. Rashi – commenting on *ḥazru vehodu,* "they acknowledged the first commandments" – states: "All the more so is one obligated to honor God, for He too is a partner in man's creation together with his father and mother; and his life and death are in His hands."[8] This

7. דרש עולה רבה אפיתחא דבי נשיאה: מאי דכתיב יוֹדוּךָ ה׳ כָּל מַלְכֵי אָרֶץ כִּי שָׁמְעוּ אִמְרֵי פִיךָ (תהלים קלח, ד)? "מאמר פיך" לא נאמר, אלא "אמרי פיך". בשעה שאמר הקב"ה אָנֹכִי ולֹא יִהְיֶה לְךָ, אמרו אומות העולם: לכבוד עצמו הוא דורש. כיון שאמר כַּבֵּד אֶת אָבִיךָ וְאֶת אִמֶּךָ – חזרו והודו למאמרות הראשונות (קידושין לא, א).

8. כל שכן שחייב אדם בכבודו, שאף הוא שותף בבריאתו כאביו ואמו, וחייו ומותו מסורין בידו (רש"י, קידושין לא, א).

is different than seeing here the complete inseparability of the ethical norm from the act of faith.[9]

Let me return to the Bartenura's tantalizing assertion that *Pirkei Avot* is not founded upon, has no relation to, a single mitzvah of the mitzvot of the Torah. That is an overwhelming statement, and it seems to fly in the face of the evidence. As I said earlier, everyone would immediately point to the mitzvah of *vehalakhta bidrakhav*, "and you shall walk in His ways." The Rambam in the first chapter of *Hilkhot De'ot*, "Laws Concerning Ethical Dispositions," presents the entire system of Jewish ethics, which is so comprehensive, as founded upon this very mitzvah of *vehalakhta bidrakhav*, "and you shall walk in His ways."

We must, I think, reinterpret the comment of the Bartenura to mean the following: These *mussarim and middot*, these ethical precepts, are unlike all other mitzvot. The mitzvah of *vehalakhta bidrakhav*, of walking in the ways of God, of imitating God, is unlike eating matzah on the fifteenth day of Nissan or blowing shofar on the first day of Tishrei or entering the *sukkah*. But how are they unlike? What is the main difference between these ethical precepts, the *mussarim and middot* in *Pirkei Avot*, and the other mitzvot? They differ in that they defy quantification; you cannot write a complete *Shulḥan Arukh* about *mussarim and middot*. When the Bartenura states, *einah meyusedet*, "not founded upon," I would add in brackets, not founded *completely* upon an explanation of any of the mitzvot, because these ethical precepts defy the normal method of legislation since they defy quantification. In fulfilling the mitzvah of eating matzah, you know exactly how much to eat – *kazayit*, the size of an olive. If you eat less you have not fulfilled the mitzvah; if you eat more there are no extra points. The mitzvah is performed in a clearly delimited, quantifiable manner. You eat a *kazayit* of matzah and in that way you fulfill the mitzvah to eat matzah on the night of the fifteenth.

Ethical perfection, on the other hand, is open-ended. It is dependent upon each individual – on one's knowledge, sensitivity, and on one's determination to remain focused on the goal and unrelentingly advance toward it.

---

9. The same is true regarding Rava's statement in the continuation of the Gemara in Kiddushin.

This principle can be demonstrated by relation to some mitzvot within the count of *taryag,* 613, which already teach us this principle. For example, the mitzvah of *tzedakah* – charity, philanthropy – cannot be uniformly quantified. *Tzedakah* is *kefi koḥo,* to the best of one's ability, and if you do more you have performed a greater mitzvah.[10] Studying Torah is another example. The mitzvah of *talmud Torah* spans a tremendous spectrum; from the minimal – the saying of *kri'at Shema* in the morning and evening – to the way R. Akiva Eiger and the Sokhatchover Rebbe, the Avnei Nezer, fulfilled the mitzvah of *talmud Torah.* This mitzvah cannot be quantified; there is no way that one can say how to fulfill it. The same is true for *gemilut ḥasadim,* acts of benevolence.[11]

There is another Gemara in Kiddushin that can help us understand this principle. The Gemara says:

> When R. Yosef would hear the sound of his mother's footsteps, he would stand up and would say: I want to stand because the *Shekhinah,* the Divine Presence, is approaching.[12]

That was his conception of how to honor his father and mother.

The Gemara continues, "R. Yoḥanan said: Fortunate is the person who never saw his father and mother."[13] This is an overwhelming statement! Its explanation according to Rashi is that this is a mitzvah which is impossible to completely fulfill.[14]

Why then did God issue such a commandment? We know that the Torah was not given to angels but was intended for ordinary people, and everything in the Torah can be fulfilled. That was the mistake of modern Jews, to think that the Torah was not intended for the modern

---

10. See Rabbi Twersky's "Some Aspects of the Jewish Attitude Toward the Welfare State," *Tradition* 5 (1963), 137–158, reprinted in his *Studies in Jewish Law and Philosophy* (Ktav, 1982), 108–129.
11. See below, pp. 75 and 92, for further discussion of *kefi koḥo* in other mitzvot. See also *Torah of the Mind* (p. 3, n. 3), 133–138 and n. 94.
12. רב יוסף כי הוה שמע קל כרעא דאמיה אמר: איקום מקמי שכינה דאתיא. (קידושין לא, ב)
13. אמר רבי יוחנן: אשרי מי שלא חמאן. (שם)
14. שאי אפשר לקיים כבודם ככל הצורך. (רש"י שם)

age. The Torah was given to us, to average human beings, and everything in the Torah can be fulfilled, all 613 mitzvot.

It is thus significant that the mitzvah of honoring one's father and mother was the mitzvah which, according to Ulah's homily, caused the nations of the world to reconsider and to acknowledge the true perspective on ethical theory. Not only is the mitzvah significant in and of itself, but it teaches an important ethical principle: if it is not possible to fulfill a mitzvah completely, even a fragmentary, partial fulfillment is meaningful.

There is here the concept of infinity in mitzvot; a person fulfilling a mitzvah is constantly running toward the boundary but never reaching it. You can come closer and closer, but you are only approximating what the mitzvah stands for. This itself is nonetheless a constructive, meaningful act; it is not a reason for frustration, and it should not yield a sense of futility. Futility means that you start out to do something and you do not succeed in accomplishing it. That can be so in certain material areas perhaps, but in the spiritual realm, the realm of mitzvot, even a partial fulfillment is noteworthy. The effort itself to fulfill a mitzvah is significant – *lefum tza'ara agra,* one is rewarded according to the effort expended.[15] This resolves the question of why this mitzvah of honoring one's parents was given at all if, as Rashi says, it is not possible to completely fulfill it. Maybe it is not possible in full measure, but as much as one does, he has fulfilled a mitzvah. The mitzvah stretches our spiritual capacity and our moral aptitude.

RAISE UP MANY DISCIPLES

Many of the principles in this special tractate of Avot are of this kind in that they are not subject to formal legislation and there is no resultant normative formulation. They reflect a creative, fluid dimension of one's religious regimen. Of the threefold maxim of *Anshei Knesset Hagedolah,* the Men of the Great Assembly,[16] I have chosen to discuss the middle statement, *ha'amidu talmidim harbeh,* "raise up many disciples," for it is the main pillar of the three statements.

15. Avot 5:26.

16. הוו מתונים בדין, והעמידו תלמידים הרבה, ועשו סייג לתורה. (אבות א, א)

Ha'amidu talmidim harbeh – raise up many students, many disciples. This idea – teach many students – seems so simple, so straightforward that we could end our *shiur* right now. And yet it is extremely complex and elusive. Already in *Avot Derabbi Natan* we find recorded a controversy between Beit Shammai and Beit Hillel.

> Raise up many disciples: Beit Shammai says, one should only teach a person who is wise, humble, of distinguished pedigree, and affluent (*it is a very restricted, aristocratic, view*). Beit Hillel says, teach everybody (*because the redemptive, cathartic power of Torah is tremendous and unpredictable*). There were many sinners, many people who had gone astray, who were then brought close to the study of Torah; they became upright people, people of great integrity and great piety.[17]

One thing is clear: Beit Shammai did not feel bound by the halakhah of the *Anshei Knesset Hagedolah*. When we read their statement *ha'amidu talmidim harbeh,* "raise up many disciples," we understand it as a halakhic decision, something that makes its way into the *Shulḥan Arukh*. But Beit Shammai still felt that they could so restrict and reinterpret the statement that there is very little resemblance between what they said and *ha'amidu talmidim harbeh,* and hence one of the basic controversies between Beit Hillel and Beit Shammai could emerge.

It is interesting that even after this disagreement between Beit Hillel and Beit Shammai – and one would assume that the halakhah would have been decided like Beit Hillel – the Gemara in Berakhot tells us that these divergent views surfaced again in the dramatic confrontation between Rabban Gamliel and his critics represented by R. Elazar ben Azaryah. The Gemara describes the uprising in the *beit midrash* against Rabban Gamliel, and it was because of this issue, whether the view of Beit Hillel or that of Beit Shammai in *ha'amidu talmidim harbeh* should be followed. The Gemara tells us:

---

17. שבית שמאי אומרים: שֶׁאל ישנה אדם אלא למי שהוא חכם עניו ובן אבות ועשיר. בית הלל אומרים: לכל אדם ישנה, שהרבה פושעים היו בהם בישראל ונתקרבו לתלמוד תורה ויצאו מהם צדיקים, חסידים וכשרים (**אבות דרבי נתן** נוסחא א, פרק ג).

> That very day they removed the guard (*the person who checked credentials*). The doors were thrown open and whoever wanted to study (*whoever was thirsting for dvar Hashem, the word of God*), could find his way in to the *beit midrash*. For Rabban Gamliel's position had been that any student about whom we see that *ein tokho kevaro* was prohibited from entering the *beit midrash*.[18]

Permission now was given to these many potential students who were eager to learn, to enter the *beit midrash*. That symbolized the victory of R. Elazar ben Azaryah and his associates over the aristocratic view of Rabban Gamliel.

Rabban Gamliel's approach had been restrictive. The term *she'ein tokho kevaro* means "about whom there is any ambiguity." There may be some discrepancy of which we are not aware, between what strikes us, what we see, and what is really the essence of this person. Since Rabban Gamliel wanted to avoid that kind of ambiguity, he would not allow them to enter; the credentials had to be carefully examined. There was a very rigorous admissions policy.

This now changed. Rabban Gamliel's policy was rejected, and on that day, the day of his dismissal and the installation of R. Elazar ben Azaryah as the *nasi*, the head of the Sanhedrin, the Gemara says, "many benches were added to the *beit midrash*." There was a dramatic upsurge in attendance. According to one report, four hundred new benches were brought into the *beit midrash*; according to another it was seven hundred.[19]

What is striking is that the Gemara then adds: *ka ḥalsha da'atei derabban Gamliel.* Rabban Gamliel did not know what to make of this; he felt faint, taken aback, and said *dilma ḥas veshalom, mana'ati Torah miyisrael,* "perhaps, God forbid, I have prevented people from studying Torah."[20] What does this mean? Did he not know that he was preventing people from studying Torah? There was a guard at the door who

---

18. אותו היום, סלקוהו לשומר הפתח ונתנה להם רשות לתלמידים ליכנס. שהיה רבן גמליאל אומר: "כל תלמיד שאין תוכו כברו לא יכנס לבית המדרש" (ברכות כח, א).

19. ההוא יומא אתוספו כמה ספסלי. אמר רבי יוחנן: "פליגי בה אבא יוסף בן דוסתאי ורבנן, חד אמר: אתוספו ארבע מאה ספסלי; וחד אמר: שבע מאה ספסלי" (שם).

20. הוה קא חלשא דעתיה דרבן גמליאל. אמר: "דלמא חס ושלום מנעתי תורה מישראל". (שם)

checked credentials, and only then was it possible to come into the *beit midrash* to hear the *shiur*!

The Gemara is telling us that Rabban Gamliel apparently thought there was a consensus about disseminating Torah and that he was walking in the footsteps of the *Anshei Knesset Hagedolah,* who said, *ha'amidu talmidim harbeh.* That is why he reacted and said *dilma,* perhaps I am guilty of withholding Torah from Yisrael. He was very distressed.

In fact, however, there was a radical divergence between the modes of implementing the statement of *Anshei Knesset Hagedolah* to "raise up many disciples." How is it accomplished? Who is to be admitted and under what circumstances? This is what changed when R. Elazar ben Azaryah, at least for a day, unseated Rabban Gamliel.

The Rambam sees this passage in the Gemara not just as a story, an aggadah, but as a source with halakhic implications. He wrote, "Torah should be taught only to a worthy student, pleasing in his deeds, or to a *tam*."[21] The beginning of the halakhah sounds like Beit Shammai. But the addition of *tam* changes that. *Tam* here means someone about whom there is some ambiguity, and you give him the benefit of the doubt. The Rambam intends to say that if you are not sure whether or not he is worthy of being admitted to the *beit midrash,* admit him. By using the phrase "or to a *tam*" the Rambam reflects the view of Beit Hillel as understood by R. Elazar ben Azaryah, who changed the rule *be'oto yom,* on that well-known day on which the uprising in the *beit midrash* took place.

This divergence in the application of "raise up many disciples" continued until modern times. If you look at the development of the yeshivot in Eastern Europe, you will find that these competing views were still fighting for supremacy. There is a parallel development in Ḥasidism. Let me present a few lines of the Sfat Emet, the great exponent of the ḥasidic movement of Ger. This is an exceptional passage that I have not seen quoted elsewhere. It is a remarkable historical-philosophical characterization of two approaches which we know existed – the approaches of Beit Shammai and Beit Hillel – the elitist,

21. אין מלמדין תורה אלא לתלמיד הגון, נאה במעשיו, או לתם (**משנה תורה** הלכות תלמוד תורה ד, א).

aristocratic, restricted view and the more exoteric, democratic view. I will paraphrase the passage.[22]

The Sfat Emet said in the name of his grandfather, the Ḥiddushei Harim – the first Rebbe of Ger and a *talmid-ḥaver,* a student-colleague, of the Kotzker Rebbe – that Yosef and Yehudah represent the two types, Beit Shammai and Beit Hillel. Yosef was withdrawn and said that very few people will have access to this superior kind of *kedushah,* whereas Yehudah wanted to bring the *kedushah* to everybody.

And then he added the following remarkable oral historical report:

> I heard him (the Ḥiddushei Harim) say that our teachers were divided on the issue; some said that there should be few Ḥasidim, but of the greatest sanctity. The others wanted piety and *kedushah* to spread among everybody even though they will be on a lesser level of perfection.

He is referring here – and I do not know whole volumes of history that say more than these two lines! – to the famous controversy that racked Poland in the years of the Kotzker Rebbe. The Kotzker Rebbe withdrew and said: "Give me ten people who will follow me into the wilderness and we will build a unique spiritual community." Not everybody could take that approach, that rigor. In particular, the Izhbitzer Rebbe broke away and said: "I want to bring this message of *kedushah* to thousands of people." It is to this controversy that the Sfat Emet, in his terse way of writing, is referring.

The goal of Torah is *kedushah.* That is why I mention this remarkable report by the Sfat Emet as a link in the chain of interpretations of that original statement of *Anshei Knesset Hagedolah, ha'amidu talmidim harbeh.* We see it in the disagreement of Beit Hillel and Beit Shammai, Rabban Gamliel and R. Elazar ben Azaryah, and on through history.

---

22. יש לומר על פי מה שכתב אדוני אבי זקני מורי ורבי זצלה"ה, כי בחינת יוסף היה להיות קדוש ונבדל בלתי ה׳ לבדו כמו שכתב נְזִיר אֶחָיו, ובחינת יהודה היה להביא הקדושה גם בעניני עולם הזה כמו שאמר וְאֶל עַמּוֹ תְּבִיאֶנּוּ. ושמעתי ממנו כי בזה היו מחולקין גם רבותינו נשמתן עדן, כי מהם רצו שיהיה מעט חסידים ויהיו קדושי עליונים, ומהם רצו להיות מתפשט החסידות בין רוב עם אף שיהיו פחותים במדרגה (**שפת אמת**, וישב, תרל"א).

If one looks at the thirteenth-century commentary of Rabbeinu Yonah on *Pirkei Avot,* he refers to the *maḥloket* between Beit Hillel and Beit Shammai. Apparently he felt that it was still a wide-open issue, an open-ended question.

Ha'amidu talmidim harbeh is a very challenging and demanding mitzvah to fulfill. If indeed it is a *halakhah pesukah,* a codified halakhah, it is as difficult as it is important, as rigorous as it is indispensable for *Klal Yisrael.*

It may be helpful to note some prerequisites, both ethical and intellectual, for fulfilling this halakhah enunciated by the *Anshei Knesset Hagedolah.*

PREREQUISITES FOR RAISING UP MANY DISCIPLES

Ḥesed

The first prerequisite is *ḥesed* – compassion, kindness, benign involvement in the development of others. In order to fulfill *ha'amidu talmidim harbeh,* one must believe in the people who are listening, in the people who are studying, in the people who are eager to learn. One must feel that they are worthy, that they are receptive, and that it is a proper investment of time and energy to share Torah with them and to expose them to Torah.

In a remarkable passage, the Gemara in Sukkah says:

> R. Elazar said: What is the meaning of the verse in Proverbs, "and the Torah of kindness is on her tongue"? Is there a Torah of kindness and a Torah that is not of kindness? ... there are those who say that Torah which is studied in order to teach others is a Torah of kindness; Torah that is studied not in order to teach others is not a Torah of kindness.[23]

The Gemara is saying that the verse cannot mean that there is such a thing as Torah that is not characterized by kindness, that is not related

23. אמר ר׳ אלעזר: פִּיהָ פָּתְחָה בְחָכְמָה וְתוֹרַת חֶסֶד עַל לְשׁוֹנָהּ, וכי יש תורה של חסד ויש תורה שאינה של חסד?... איכא דאמרי תורה ללמדה זו היא תורה של חסד, שלא ללמדה זו היא תורה שאינה של חסד (סוכה מט, ב).

to *ḥesed*. That would be impossible. The content of the Torah doesn't change, and *ḥesed* is the hallmark of the Torah. It is in fact the hallmark of God, about whom it is said, "The Lord is good to all, and His compassion extends to all His works."[24] Thus, the Gemara asks its question in such wonderment because it is impossible to assume that "Torah of kindness and Torah that is not of kindness" can be understood from the vantage point of the content, for Torah is always, immutably, a *Torah shel ḥesed,* a Torah of kindness. What the Gemara says is that one can speak of *Torah shel ḥesed* and *Torah she'einah shel ḥesed,* a Torah of kindness and a Torah that is not characterized by kindness, in terms of transmission, in terms of teaching, in terms of your relation to Torah and to others who should be exposed to the Torah.

One can acquire a vast knowledge of Torah, but if the intention is not to teach and share with others, it is *Torah she'einah shel ḥesed,* a Torah that is not characterized by kindness. This is striking proof and illustration of the first prerequisite, that *Torah* must be *shel ḥesed* and thus should be studied in order to transmit the Torah, in order to teach Torah – to have faith that the teaching is worthwhile and that the transmission of Torah is effective.

The *Sifrei* in *Ha'azinu*[25] comments on the words *Kel emunah*: God had faith in creation, He identified with the world and therefore He invested in it. *Torah shel ḥesed* is the same: we have faith in all those who want to be exposed to Torah, and therefore devote time and intellectual-spiritual resources to them.

Tzniut – Humility

A second prerequisite for *ha'amidu talmidim harbeh* is *tzniut,* humility – an inner-directed quality that frees one from all pompousness and officiousness, that helps rid one of artificiality and pretense – and if you see the image of the Rov in front of you, that is exactly what I have in

24. טוֹב ה׳ לַכֹּל וְרַחֲמָיו עַל כָּל מַעֲשָׂיו (תהלים קמה, ט); עיינו הלכות מלכים י, יב – ״אפילו הגויים צוו חכמים לבקר חוליהם, ולקבור מתיהם עם מתי ישראל, ולפרנס ענייהם בכלל עניי ישראל, מפני דרכי שלום; הרי נאמר טוֹב ה׳ לַכֹּל וְרַחֲמָיו עַל כָּל מַעֲשָׂיו, ונאמר דְּרָכֶיהָ דַרְכֵי נֹעַם וְכָל נְתִיבֹתֶיהָ שָׁלוֹם״. ועיינו גם סוף הלכות עבדים.

25. קֵל אֱמוּנָה, שהאמין בעולם ובראו. (**ספרי על ספר דברים** פיסקא שז, ד)

mind. A proud, condescending, self-centered person who ponders every step and every gesture, no matter how learned, will not be influential and successful as a transmitter of the *masorah,* as a master of Torah. You must bring yourself to the level of intelligent, inspiring communication with everyone who is eager to advance and to acquire learning. Proper teaching satisfies and stimulates at the same time. Above all, a teacher of Torah must never exhibit learning or piety indiscriminately. Some people wear their modest measure of learning or their *yir'at shamayim,* their fear of Heaven, as an outer garment; they parade it and flaunt it for no purpose.

The Gemara in Mo'ed Katan[26] tells us that once Rebbe, R. Yehudah Hanasi, decreed that the students should not go out and teach Torah in the marketplace, in the public square. He was emphasizing the need for *tzniut,* humility. The Gemara then says that R. Ḥiyya, the leading student of Rebbe, disobeyed this teaching. He went out and taught the sons of his two brothers in the open marketplace. Rebbe heard of this and was angry. Word reached R. Ḥiyya that Rebbe was angry, and R. Ḥiyya realized that he must act as if he had been banned. For thirty days he conducted himself as if he were in *nidui,* excommunication.

The Gemara then tells us that Rebbe called him at the end of the thirty days and asked: "Why did you behave in the way that you did?" R. Ḥiyya answered him: "I thought that this was the meaning of the verse at the beginning of Proverbs, 'Wisdom cries aloud in the street.' I thought this means that you had to go public and show your wisdom, your Torah." Rebbe chastised him and said: "If you read this verse once, you didn't review it a second time; and if you read it a second time you didn't look at it a third time; and even if you did try to understand it a third time, you did not receive the correct interpretation. You were lacking a *masorah,* you were trying on your own, with your own understanding, to figure out what is the application of *Ḥokhmot baḥutz taronah,* 'Wisdom cries

26. גזר רבי שלא ישנו לתלמידים בשוק. מאי דרש? חַמּוּקֵי יְרֵכַיִךְ כְּמוֹ חֲלָאִים (שיר השרים ז, ב), מה ירך בסתר אף דברי תורה בסתר. יצא רבי חייא ושנה לשני בני אחיו בשוק... שמע רבי – איקפד... נהג נזיפותא בנפשיה תלתין יומין. ביום תלתין שלח ליה... מאי טעמא עבד מר הכי? – אמר ליה: דכתיב חָכְמוֹת בַּחוּץ תָּרֹנָּה (משלי א, כ). אמר ליה: אם קרית – לא שנית, ואם שנית – לא שילשת, ואם שילשת – לא פירשו לך. חָכְמוֹת בַּחוּץ תָּרֹנָּה – כדרבא. דאמר רבא: כל העוסק בתורה מבפנים – תורתו מכרזת עליו מבחוץ (מועד קטן טז, א–ב).

aloud in the street.'" Rebbe told him that he totally missed the intent of this verse because he lacked a *masorah,* the proper traditional insight here, and that *Ḥokhmot baḥutz taronah* has to be understood as Rava explained it. Rava said: If one studies the Torah *mibifnim,* that is, with humility, with the attitude and modality of *tzniut,* then the Torah proclaims his merit abroad, in public. You do not have to ring your own bell if you study Torah sincerely and modestly.

This is what I mean by the second prerequisite or the second trait for raising up many disciples – *tzniut,* humility. R. Ḥiyya was censured for publicizing Torah aimlessly. Rebbe wanted him to understand that one should not parade Torah scholarship without a clear pedagogic purpose or some moral spiritual objective.

The Yerushalmi in Berakhot[27] indeed interprets the verse in Proverbs, "*ve'et tznuim ḥokhmah,*" to mean that wisdom, knowledge of the Torah, is to be acquired with an inner-directed humility. And the Rambam quotes this very verse in *Hilkhot Talmud Torah*[28] insisting that *talmudo,* one's knowledge of Torah, is acquired through *tzniut,* which is a prerequisite for studying, acquiring knowledge, and transmitting it.

There are many reasons for the importance of *tzniut* in the study of Torah, and I will briefly mention two of them.

The Gemara in Sotah tells us that God cannot dwell in the same place as a proud, condescending person: "Any person who has arrogance within him, the Holy One, blessed be He, said: He and I cannot dwell together in the world."[29] The world is not big enough for God and a *ba'al ga'avah,* an arrogant person. The *ba'al ga'avah* thinks he is too expansive, and thus there is no room for God. *Pirkei Avot* teaches us repeatedly that God accompanies the Torah; God is found where Torah is studied. In the Rov's writings there are many dramatic descriptions of this experience,[30] of being together with God's Torah while engaged in the

27. ברית כרותה היא, היגע תלמודו בצנעה לא במהרה הוא משכח. מה טעם? וְאֶת צְנוּעִים חָכְמָה (משלי יא, ב; תלמוד ירושלמי ברכות ה, א).

28. וכל היגע בתלמודו בצנעה מחכים, שנאמר וְאֶת צְנוּעִים חָכְמָה (**משנה תורה** הלכות תלמוד תורה, ג, יב).

29. כל אדם שיש בו גסות הרוח, אמר הקב"ה, אין אני והוא יכולים לדור בעולם. (סוטה ה, א)

30. [See, e.g., Rabbi Joseph B. Soloveitchik, *And from There You Shall Seek,* trans. Naomi Goldblum (Ktav, 2003), 143–146; idem *On Repentance,* ed. Pinchas Peli (Paulist

act of study. It is thus not just an intellectual undertaking; therefore the need for humility, for *tzniut*.

A second reason for the importance of *tzniut* is due to the fact that the *ḥakham*, the learned person, must share the trait of the *ḥokhmah*, the wisdom, which is being studied. The wisdom of the Torah is something that is intrinsically great and worthy, something that doesn't have to be flaunted; there is no need for any ostentation. If you are fully convinced of its value and of its truth, there is no need for any extraneous or artificial validation. This is the essence of Torah. If one wants to relate to this precious commodity of Torah – which is characterized as a *kli tzanu'a*, a humble vessel[31] described most succinctly and emblematically by *tzniut* – then you have to share that trait.

Self-Confidence and Independence

A third prerequisite for *ha'amidu talmidim harbeh* is that there must be an effort to instill self-confidence in the students of Torah, in the *talmidim*. Colloquially this idea is expressed as ***ha'amidu*** *talmidim* – literally, raise up, i.e., let them stand on their own two feet. The teacher should help the *talmidim* achieve independence by elevating them and encouraging them to develop, and not to remain dependent, both intellectually and spiritually. In the sixth chapter of Avot we find: "Whoever regularly occupies himself with the study of the Torah, he is surely exalted";[32] that is, the process of study should elevate the person. The job of the teacher is to develop one's religious consciousness while fully engaging the mind as well.

An illustration of this can be found in the Gemara in Bava Batra: "One who has a sick person in his house should go to a wise man and *yevakesh alav raḥamim*, he will ask for mercy."[33] Who is the subject of *yevakesh*? Who will ask or pray, and for whom? Now this would sound like a *ḥasidishe Gemara*, a Gemara with a ḥasidic orientation. But this is not so. This does not mean that you should ask the *ḥakham* to pray

Press, 1984), 142.]

31. Ta'anit 16a.

32. כל מי שעוסק בתלמוד תורה הרי זה מתעלה. (אבות ו, ב)

33. כל שיש לו חולה בתוך ביתו, ילך אצל חכם ויבקש עליו רחמים. (בבא בתרא קטז, א)

for you (or for the sick person in your house). The Meiri explains the Gemara in the following way:

> A person should have no doubt that sincere, meaningful prayer is effective and achieves its goal. And if a person suffers from any adversity (such as having a sick person in his household, or other types of adversity), he should learn from the *ḥakham* how to pray properly. Then this needy, distraught person, the one suffering from adversity, should pray for himself.[34]

That is the mandate and function of a *ḥakham*: to enable the other, the student, to act correctly, with independence, and not to perpetuate a state of dependence.

The best *talmidim* in the Gemara are described as *talmidim* who have something to contribute to the development of the teacher, as the Gemara in Ḥagigah says: "A *talmid* who increases the wisdom of his teachers,"[35] or as the Gemara in Menaḥot says: A *talmid* who helps bring precision and clarity to a *shmu'a*, to a halakhah.[36]

On the other hand, *talmidim* always have something to learn from a rebbe. The Rov often would wonder why certain rabbis didn't call with halakhic questions. This was not because he wanted to perpetuate dependence, but rather he felt that this was how they would continue to learn and develop.

All of this is part of *ha'amidu talmidim harbeh*, raise up many disciples.

THE PRESERVATION OF THE *MASORAH*

The real significance of *ha'amidu talmidim harbeh*, the reason why it is indispensable and is the central pillar of the teachings of the *Anshei*

---

34. לעולם יהא לבו של אדם בטוח שהתפלה כשהיא נעשית כתקנה מבטלת את הגזרה. ומי שיש לו צער או חולה בתוך ביתו, או אחד ממיני הצרות, ילך אצל חכם **וילמוד הימנו דרכי התפלות ויבקש רחמים** (ר׳ מנחם המאירי, **בית הבחירה** על בבא בתרא קט״, א).

35. תלמיד המחכיב את רבותיו. (חגיגה יד, א)

36. אמר לו: יוסף, כמדומה אני שלא כיוונו שמועתיו עד עתה. (מנחות יח, א)

Knesset Hagedolah, is that the essence of *talmud Torah,* the essence of the study of Torah, is the transmission and the preservation of the *masorah.*

Ḥazal see *veshinnantam levanekha,* "you shall teach your sons diligently,"[37] as a key to understanding the centrality of the *masorah*'s preservation. This is evident in the triple interpretation that they offer for this phrase. The first is found in the *Sifrei,* where they explicate *veshinnantam levanekha* to mean *elu talmidekha,* these are your students.[38] In other words, the obligation to teach Torah is not only to one's own children, as the literal meaning of the verse implies, but it also requires perpetuating the *masorah* by expanding the obligation to teach Torah beyond the family circle. Not only must a father teach his children, but the wise and the learned are obliged to teach Torah to all. Thus, when the Midrash identifies *banekha* with *talmidekha,* it imposes upon all learned individuals the obligation to teach all students.

The Rambam incorporates this interpretation into the very beginning of *Hilkhot Talmud Torah.*[39]

The Gemara in Kiddushin, which details methodology of the perpetuation of the *masorah,* adds two further interpretations of the verse.

The first is:

> R. Safra says in the name of R. Yehoshua ben Ḥananya: What is the meaning of that which is written: "And you shall teach them diligently [*veshinnantam*] to your sons"? Do not read this as *veshinnantam*; rather, read it as *veshillashtam.*[40]

The Gemara explains that you are to divide your studies into three parts: one third the written Torah, one third the Mishnah, and one

---

37. Devarim 6:7.

38. "ושננתם לבניך" – אלו תלמידך. (**ספרי על ספר דברים ואתחנן לד**)

39. כשם שחייב אדם ללמד את בנו, כך הוא חייב ללמד את בן בנו, שנאמר: וְהוֹדַעְתָּם לְבָנֶיךָ וְלִבְנֵי בָנֶיךָ. ולא בנו ובן בנו בלבד אלא מצוה על כל חכם וחכם מישראל ללמד את כל התלמידים אף על פי שאינן בניו, שנאמר וְשִׁנַּנְתָּם לְבָנֶיךָ; מפי השמועה למדו בניך, אלו תלמידיך, שהתלמידים קרויין בנים (**משנה תורה** הלכות תלמוד תורה א, ב).

40. אמר רב ספרא משום ר׳ יהושע בן חנניה: מאי דכתיב: וְשִׁנַּנְתָּם לְבָנֶיךָ? אל תקרי ושננתם אלא ושלשתם, לעולם ישלש אדם שנותיו, שליש במקרא, שליש במשנה, שליש בתלמוד (קידושין ל, א).

third Talmud, thereby encompassing all aspects of Torah, striving for comprehensiveness.[41] Knowledge is not limited to the written Torah but must embrace the *masorah* in its entirety. The importance of this is expressed by the fact that even if you want to teach a verse of *Ḥumash* and Rashi properly in the fifth grade, you need to know so much more than just fifth-grade level *Ḥumash*. This is probably more demanding than to explain a difficult Rambam on the post-graduate level.

The second interpretation of *Ḥazal* in Kiddushin is:

> The Sages taught: "And you shall teach them diligently [*veshinnantam*]" – that matters of Torah should be *meḥudadim befikha*, sharp in your mouth, so that if a person asks you something, do not answer him with a stutter; rather, answer him immediately.[42]

Meḥudadim befikha means that your grasp of Torah should be precise, sharp, so that when you are called upon to expound something, you should do it with maximum clarity. Clarity of understanding makes possible the clarity of transmission, of exposition. I have always felt that *sheyihiyu meḥudadim befikha* could well be the slogan or motto of Brisk. The Torah had to be presented with the greatest conceptual precision and rigor. I remember being told many times (in different tones of voice) in the name of Reb Ḥayyim that if you needed five words to explain something do not use four and do not use six. That is precision, and that precision reflects clarity of understanding that makes possible clarity of transmission.

The latter two interpretations in Kiddushin provide the guidelines for fulfilling the first understanding of *veshinnantam levanekha*, that of the *Sifrei*, which is the mitzvah of *levanekha, elu talmidekha*. It is your obligation to teach all of your disciples in a comprehensive manner with precision and with clarity.

---

41. See pp. 117–118 for an expanded analysis of this passage. See too R. Twersky's *Introduction to the Code of Maimonides* (*Mishneh Torah*) (Yale University Press, 1980), ch. 3, for a full analysis of comprehensiveness in Maimonides' writing, as well as the background for this approach before his time.

42. ת"ר, וְשִׁנַּנְתָּם שיהו דברי תורה מחודדים בפיך. שאם ישאל לך אדם דבר אל תגמגם ותאמר לו, אלא אמור לו מיד (שם).

EXPERIENCING TORAH

This comprehensiveness in the teaching of Torah must include a personal dimension as well. The teacher must share his own emotional-experiential components of Torah. They are his own emotions, his personal experience of a certain mitzvah, but he has to share these. He must help the students penetrate to what is called the *nishmat hatorah,* the soul of the Torah.

We find this emphasis from the period of the *Rishonim* and on. The Ramban emphasized this experiential element of *talmud Torah,* and throughout the generations we find the terms *nishmat hatorah* and *penimiyut hatorah* to express the idea of the inner essence of Torah.[43]

The Ramban's discussion of the inner essence of Torah is to be found in his critique of the Rambam in the *Sefer Hamitzvot.* The Ramban notes that the Rambam omits a very important *lo ta'aseh,* negative commandment, in his count of mitzvot. The basis of Ramban's argument is a verse in Devarim, *hishamer lekha … pen tishkaḥ et hadevarim asher ra'u einekha,*[44] which the Ramban interprets literally to mean: "Take heed, be careful, lest you forget the things which your eyes beheld." Rashi says, and apparently the Rambam understood it as Rashi did, that "lest you forget the things which your eyes beheld" refers to the content of revelation, that is, the mitzvot. The Ramban, however, is of the opinion that it refers not to the content of the mitzvot but rather to the circumstances, to the experience of receiving the Torah. It refers to the excitement, the exhilaration, the encounter with God that accompanied and continues to accompany the study of Torah and the performance of mitzvot. All this can be summarized in the words *ma'amad Har Sinai,* the very experience of being present at Mount Sinai when the Torah was given. The Ramban thus lists this mitzvah as one of those that the Rambam forgot to include in his count of the mitzvot.

43. Thus R. Ḥayyim of Volozhin in his *Nefesh Haḥayyim* and in other works speaks of *penimiyut hatorah* and *nishmat hatorah* [עיין למשל **נפש החיים** א, טז: ועל ידי כך זכו להשיג סתרי פנימיות נשמת התורה הקדושה].

44. הִשָּׁמֶר לְךָ וּשְׁמֹר נַפְשְׁךָ מְאֹד פֶּן תִּשְׁכַּח אֶת הַדְּבָרִים אֲשֶׁר רָאוּ עֵינֶיךָ וּפֶן יָסוּרוּ מִלְּבָבְךָ כֹּל יְמֵי חַיֶּיךָ וְהוֹדַעְתָּם לְבָנֶיךָ וְלִבְנֵי בָנֶיךָ. יוֹם אֲשֶׁר עָמַדְתָּ לִפְנֵי ה׳ אֱלֹקֶיךָ בְּחֹרֵב ... (דברים ד, ט–י).

The Ramban, however, is puzzled by why the Rambam did not realize this, and he tries to reconstruct the Rambam's position on the issue. He suggests[45] that one could have been misled by a passage in Kiddushin that says, "When one teaches his grandchildren Torah, it is as if he received it at Mount Sinai."[46] The verse used in the Gemara to prove this is the very verse that the Ramban cited to prove that the prohibition of forgetting the experience of receiving the Torah is a negative command, i.e., *hishamer lekha… pen tishkaḥ et hadevarim asher ra'u einekha,* the verse in Deuteronomy just cited above. The conclusion of the verse reads, *vehodatam levanekha velivnei vanekha,* "And you shall make them known to your children and to your children's children."[47] This is the very proof text that the Rambam uses to support the obligation to teach Torah to your son, grandson, and all your students, and from the context it is clear that the Rambam is discussing teaching the content of Torah, the halakhot of the Torah, to one's descendants.[48] Ramban, however, asserts that this is not the proper interpretation of the verse. It refers to something else entirely: to communicate to our children, descendants, and students the *experience* of the mitzvot, not their content.

Then, with a special emphasis that resonated throughout the generations, the Ramban continues: "Studying about the belief in Torah is itself the study of Torah."[49] Do not think that only by studying strictly halakhic matters, such as the counting of the *omer,* does one fulfill the mitzvah of studying Torah. Not only is studying about the belief in Torah considered the study of Torah, but it is the *basis* of Torah. The transmission of the truth about the tradition is indispensable for the transmission

---

45. ואל תטעה בזה מפני דורשם בראשון של קידושין (ל, א) לְבָנֶיךָ וְלִבְנֵי בָנֶיךָ בלימוד התורה לבני בנים. **כי לימוד אמונת התורה הוא הלימוד בתורה.** אבל נתבונן ונקח ראיה מדבריהם כי היא מצוה עולמית, ועם כל הדורות ידבר, שלא ישכחו ענין המעמד ההוא שהיה לכל העם במראית עיניהם ושמיעת אזניהם, ושיעתיקו זה מדור לדור לעולם (**ספר המצוות להרמב"ם עם השגות הרמב"ן**, מהדורת חיים דב שעוועל, מוסד הרב קוק, תשמ"א, השכחה מן הרב במצוה לא תעשה, המצווה הב׳, עמ׳ שצו).

46. אמר ר׳ יהושע בן לוי: כל המלמד את בן בנו תורה, מעלה עליו הכתוב כאילו קבלה מהר סיני, שנאמר: וְהוֹדַעְתָּם לְבָנֶיךָ וְלִבְנֵי בָנֶיךָ, וסמיך ליה: יוֹם אֲשֶׁר עָמַדְתָּ לִפְנֵי ה' אֱלֹקֶיךָ בְּחֹרֵב (קידושין ל, א).

47. See n. 44 above.

48. See n. 39 above.

49. Cited in n. 45 above.

of the tradition itself, of the content of the tradition. The latter would be lost if divorced from the truth about the *masorah.*

Thus, *ha'amidu talmidim harbeh* must include this effort on the part of the teacher to help his students understand *nishmat hatorah,* the inner experience of Torah, to teach all forty-eight traits that the Mishnah in the sixth chapter of Avot tells us are necessary for studying Torah. They are both prerequisites for and results of learning Torah.

This truth is frequently forgotten, and this caused the Rov much anguish of soul. I have a letter he wrote to me in the summer of 1969, when I was in Yerushalayim, about his experience of *ha'amidu talmidim harbeh,* of teaching Gemara, and of his great disappointment of trying to teach *nishmat hatorah.*[50]

This helps us understand the personal dimension of the *masorah* in general, and the moral, subjective, experiential dimension of the *masorah* as embodied, for example, in *Pirkei Avot.* This *masorah* is transmitted privately – not publicly, as is the Halakhah in toto – and that is why the phrase *Hu hayah omer,* "He was known to say," is the slogan of *Pirkei Avot.* The fact that he said it privately, and behaved accordingly, became the basis of a commandment. He didn't have to teach it publicly as law. "He was known to say" means his personality, his behavior, his very being communicated the teaching to others and urged them to adopt this precept and this precedent. This represents a special kind of *masorah,* a *masorah* of observation, not one of teaching and analysis.

The importance of personal observation for the perpetuation of the *masorah* can be exemplified by the halakhah of counting the *omer,* which begins on the day after the first day of Pesaḥ. The Rambam emphasizes that this is known *mipi hashmu'ah,* by oral tradition.[51] And

50. [See also the similar comments of the Rov:
"על אהבת התורה וגאולת נפש הדור", **בסוד היחוד והיחד**, בעריכת פנחס פלאי, אורות, תשל"ו, עמ' 407-417. "כי לצעירים החרדים התגלתה התורה בצורות מחשבה למדנית, בהכרה שכלית והיגיון צונן. אולם לא זכו לגילויה בהרגשה ה'חושית' החיה, המרעידה והמרנינה לבבות. מכירים המה את התורה כאידיאה, אבל אינם נפגשים עמה כ'מציאות' בלתי־אמצעית הנרגשת ב'טעם מראה ומישוש'" (שם עמ' 407-408).]

51. מפני אלו הטועים שיצאו מכלל ישראל בבית שני, שהן אומרין שזה שנאמר בתורה ממחרת השבת הוא שבת בראשית. ומפי השמועה למדו שאינה שבת אלא יום טוב; וכן **ראו** תמיד הנביאים והסנהדרין בכל דור ודור (**משנה תורה** הלכות תמידין ומוספין ז, יא).

how did they know this? The prophets saw – I would emphasize *ra'u,* they saw, they observed. The prophets and the Sages of the Sanhedrin saw that this was the practice generation after generation. You do not need any intellectual subtlety to know when to perform the mitzvah of *sefirat ha'omer,* the counting of the *omer,* because there exists a *masorah* of observation, of actual seeing. Just as there is a *masorah,* a tradition, of *talmud Torah,* of analysis, and of *shimush,* serving Torah scholars, here you have, in addition, a *masorah* of observation.

This *masorah* of actual observation relates not only to the specific teachings but to the persona of the teacher as well. The Gemara in Eiruvin says that Rebbe, R. Yehudah Hanasi, who formulated the basis of our entire Oral Law, *Torah sheb'al peh,* said that he achieved distinction because he observed R. Meir. But he adds that "I only got a rear view, a glimpse of him; had I seen him frontally, had I had a better view, then my own wisdom and Torah would have been deeper, richer, and more encompassing."[52] This does not mean only: "Had I been able to have a more sustained exposure experientially, had I seen more of his practices, I would have become more familiar with his behavioral customs." That is the meaning of *ma'aseh rav,* reporting one's teacher's personal practices. "Had I had a better view" also means that I would understand his analysis of Torah better. The two are inseparable. Had I seen him not "from the rear" but frontally – if I had known him more intimately – I would have a better understanding of his teachings as well.[53]

The scribe who recorded all the teachings of R. Naḥman of Breslov, R. Natan, states: "Happy are the eyes that looked into the eyes of R. Naḥman." That's exactly what this Gemara in Eiruvin about Rebbe and R. Meir is saying. But then R. Natan adds, "Happy are the eyes that

---

כמו כן ראו דברי הרמב"ם האלו: אע"פ שדברים אלו נראים מענין תורה שבכתב, כולן מפורשין הן מפי משה מהר סיני, וכולן הלכה למעשה הן בידינו, וכזה **ראו** אבותינו דנין בבית דינו של יהושע ובבית דינו של שמואל הרמתי ובכל בית דין ובית דין שעמדו מימות משה ועד עכשיו (**משנה תורה** הלכות חובל ומזיק א, ו).

52. אמר רבי: האי דמחדדנא מחבראי, דחזיתיה לרבי מאיר מאחוריה, ואילו חזיתיה מקמיה, הוה מחדדנא טפי דכתיב וְהָיוּ עֵינֶיךָ רֹאוֹת אֶת מוֹרֶיךָ (ישעיהו ל, כ; עירובין יג, ב).

53. For further elaboration, see p. 72.

looked into my eyes that looked into his eyes."[54] If the *masorah* is kept alive as *masorah* must be – as a personal, living, pulsating *masorah* – then one's total understanding of Torah, not just of specific matters of practice and behavior, a *minhag* here and there, is enhanced even once-removed. "Happy are the eyes that looked into my eyes that looked into his eyes" is the basis of understanding Torah on any level.

May the *zekhut*, the merit, of the Rov and the *zekhut* of his Torah protect us.

54. מוֹהַרְנַ"תְ אָמַר פַּעַם: אַשְׁרֵי הָעֵינַיִם שֶׁרָאוּ אֶת עֵינֵי רַבֵּנוּ, וְאַשְׁרֵי הָעֵינַיִם הָרוֹאוֹת אֶת הָעֵינַיִם שֶׁרָאוּ אֶת רַבֵּנוּ (**שיח שרפי קודש** חלק ב, תקלא).

ובתורתו יהגה יומם ולילה - תורה דיליה היא

Chapter 2

From God's Torah to the Scholar's Torah

"HIS" TORAH

[*Ḥazal* use the phrase *Torah dilei,* his Torah, to express the notion that the Torah, given to us by God (*His* Torah), can become the Torah of the scholar who studies it (*his* Torah). How does that process take place? What are the halakhic implications of that process? What are the qualities needed to acquire such knowledge? And finally, what are the privileges, responsibilities, and obligations of that scholar who acquires Torah?]

The first chapter in the book of Tehillim opens with the following two verses: "[1] Happy is the man who has not walked in the wicked's counsel, nor in the way of offenders has stood, nor in the session of scoffers has sat. [2] But his desire, or delight, is in the Torah of the Lord and in His (*capital H*) Torah does he meditate day and night."[1] What stands out about the translation of the second verse, representative of the way this verse is generally understood, is the assumption of

---

1. אַשְׁרֵי הָאִישׁ אֲשֶׁר לֹא הָלַךְ בַּעֲצַת רְשָׁעִים וּבְדֶרֶךְ חַטָּאִים לֹא עָמָד וּבְמוֹשַׁב לֵצִים לֹא יָשָׁב. כִּי אִם בְּתוֹרַת ה׳ חֶפְצוֹ וּבְתוֹרָתוֹ יֶהְגֶּה יוֹמָם וָלָיְלָה (תהלים א, א-ב).

parallelism. In other words, there are two halves to this verse, and the second half simply repeats, maybe extends a bit, what is said in the first half. Hence this translation assumes the identity of the first half of the verse, "The Torah of the LORD," with the second half, "His Torah." It also assumes the equivalence of "that in which one takes delight" and "that in which one meditates." This is certainly a powerful verse.

The Gemara in Avodah Zarah suggests an entirely different interpretation which adds even more power and force to the verse, and is an enthralling challenge to everybody. It says that at first the Torah is *torat Hashem*, "the Torah of the LORD," but at the end of some process – involving study, as we will see – *nikreit al shemo*, it is identified with the one who has gone through this process, *uve'torato yehegeh*, "in his (*small h*) Torah does he meditate."[2]

It is quite clear that *Ḥazal* here do not view the words *uve'torato yehegeh*, "in his Torah does he meditate," in the second half of the verse as parallel to "the Torah of the LORD" in the first half. Rather, they understand it to mean "in *his* Torah," the Torah of the one who studies, the one who has gone through the process implicit in the verse. Only then is the Torah "identified with the one who has gone through this process," only then does it become *his* Torah. Rashi explains[3] that when *Ḥazal* say *nikrait al shemo*, "identified with the one who has gone through this process," they mean the Torah is attributed to the student *shetaraḥ bah*, who invested the time and effort to acquire it. In that one phrase Rashi has summed up for us what is only alluded to but not spelled out in the verse. There is a process, as the Gemara says: *beteḥilah*, there is a beginning, and *levasof*, there is an end.[4] At the end, the ownership changes; it is no longer God's Torah, so to speak, but it becomes the student's Torah. That is Rashi's emphasis: "The Torah is now attributed to the student who invested the effort to acquire it." Then Rashi adds, "As it is written, 'In *his* Torah,'" in order to emphasize that "*his* Torah" is to be

2. ואמר רבא: בתחילה **נקראת על שמו של הקב״ה** ולבסוף **נקראת על שמו** שנאמר בְּתוֹרַת ה׳ חֶפְצוֹ **וּבְתוֹרָתוֹ** יֶהְגֶּה יוֹמָם וָלָיְלָה (עבודה זרה יט, א).

3. **נקראת על שמו:** של אותו תלמיד **שטרח בה**, כדכתיב: ״ובתורתו״, דמשמע של כל אדם (רש״י שם).

4. Note 2, above.

understood not as a repetition of "the Torah of the Lord," but rather in a new sense, as the Torah of the student.

God grants proprietary rights in His Torah to the one who studies it; the student now becomes the owner, and it is attributed to him. God's Torah becomes, if you like, everyman's Torah.

In this same Gemara, Rava immediately adds a parallel interpretation to the same verse:

> Rava says: A person must always study Torah, and then meditate upon it, as it is stated: "[His delight is] in the Torah of the Lord," and afterward: "And upon *his* Torah does he meditate."[5]

The Gemara here explicitly rejects again the interpretation that is based on parallelism, which, as I said, assumes repetition. The Gemara cites the words of Rava, "A person must always study Torah," that relate to the first half of the verse, "his delight is in the Torah of the Lord." If you are drawn to Torah, if you delight in God's Torah, you will study it and practice it; and then you will meditate upon it, you will probe in a deeper and more profound way, and the result will be that it will become your Torah. The first stage is the study of God's Torah, but when the process is completed, when you have achieved "in *his* Torah does he meditate," it will have become yours.

Rashi adds the explanation of the words "study" and "meditate": "A person should study with his teacher, and achieve fluency in the text and its interpretation."[6] "Achieving fluency" appears in the Mishnah in Berakhot, where it describes the ease with which one should be able to recite the prayers; such fluency is a good omen.[7]

Rashi in our Gemara says that "study" means to know the text of Torah well. This relates not to one's depth of understanding, but rather to reciting with ease when quoting and referring to the text. Then Rashi explains the next words of Rava's statement, "then meditate": "He

---

5. ואמר רבא: לעולם ילמד אדם תורה ואחר כך יהגה שנאמר "בתורת ה'" והדר "ובתורתו יהגה" (עבודה זרה יט, א).
6. **ילמד אדם:** מרבו עד שתהיה גירסת התלמוד ופירושו שגורה לו בפיו. (רש"י שם)
7. אם שגורה תפלתי בפי יודע אני שהוא מקובל. (משנה ברכות ה, ה)

should then delve deeply into the text, compare different cases to one another, ask questions, and suggest solutions."[8] Here Rashi presents in condensed form a description of the process of analytic study, what is sometimes called, in the positive sense, *pilpul*, in-depth study; namely, to ask a pointed question and to come up with a compelling answer. To do a comparative analysis means to compare the laws of prayer with those of studying Torah, to compare the laws of the Passover sacrifice with those of eating matzah on the night of Pesaḥ.

Rashi could have stopped here; his last comment would have sufficed to explain the terms "study" and "meditate." But Rashi was not satisfied. He appends an additional comment: "One should not start out with analytic questions, in case the teacher will have to interrupt his instruction, and will not be available later."[9]

Before explaining these last words of Rashi, I want to suggest the following, parenthetically. If you look closely at the first Rashi that begins with the words "attributed to him,"[10] you will see that Rava's second statement regarding the learning process, "A person must always study Torah, and then meditate upon it,"[11] is already alluded to in that first Rashi, when he says, "Of that student who struggled with it, who exerted himself, who applied himself unstintingly."

If you look at Rashi's commentary on the verse in Tehillim,[12] you will see that instead of the word *taraḥ* he uses the word *amal*, which we know from the phrase *hevu ameilim batorah*,[13] "Invest great effort to understand Torah." In modern Hebrew the root *amal* is used for exercise, "to work out." *Ameilim batorah* means to work out in Torah, to work your way up from achieving fluency to understanding when a question should be asked, and then to developing a proper methodology so that you will know what kind of answer to look for. All of that is compressed into Rashi's word *taraḥ*, or, as he formulates it in his commentary on Tehillim,

8. **ואחר כך יהגה:** יעיין בתלמודו, לדמות מילתא למילתא, להקשות ולתרץ (רש"י, עבודה זרה יט, א).

9. ובראשונה לא יעשה כן, שמא יבטל והרב לא ימצא לו כל שעה. (רש"י שם)

10. Note 3, above.

11. Note 5, above.

12. תחלה היא נקראת תורת ה' **ומשעמל** בה היא נקראת תורתו. (רש"י, תהלים א, ב)

13. הוו עמלים בתורה. (**ספרא**, תחילת פרשת בחקותי)

amal. Both these words mean serious systematic study which is profound and penetrating – one needs perseverance in *talmud Torah* – and which is based on love and commitment. You do not acquire rights to Torah easily. You do not acquire the ownership which is available to you without investment of your intellectual and spiritual resources. It comes with dedication, which is why the process begins with desire; there has to be love and commitment, followed by hard work. Hard work is measured by its intellectual rigor and accomplishments.

Returning to Rava: his second statement which we saw above, "A person must always study Torah, and then meditate upon it,"[14] actually underscores a necessary sequence in *talmud Torah*. Rava says, first establish solid foundations for independent study by taking advantage of your rebbe, by utilizing the learning, the resourcefulness, which are available to you in your teacher. That is what Rashi emphasizes by saying, "One should not start out with analytic questions, in case the teacher will have to interrupt his instruction, and will not be available later."[15] There are certain basic questions that one has to ask early in the process; later, it may be too late. Many can think of one question that he or she would have liked to ask the Rov – just one – but now it is too late. This is why Rashi emphasizes not to start with deep analysis; be a student, be attentive, because there will come a time when your teacher will not be available. The rebbe will not be there to instruct and to explain.

Rashi then continues:

> Furthermore, after he has extensively reviewed his studies, he reflects upon them, and is able independently to find solutions to difficult issues.[16]

Why does Rashi introduce this with "furthermore"? He is adding that this is what intellectual honesty demands. If you do it this way, you prepare yourself for independent study, you get a sense of method, you

14. See n. 5 above.

15. See n. 9 above.

16. ועוד לאחר ששנה הרבה הוא מתיישב בתלמודו ומתרץ לעצמו דבר הקשה (רש"י, עבודה זרה יט, א).

develop an intuitive grasp of the nature of the Oral Law, and then you will have the ability to come up with new insights. You have here the fusion of intellectual honesty and moral integrity; as we will see later, both are major determinants in this process of the Torah becoming "his Torah," of one's taking possession of the Torah.

Now we can go another step forward.

CONSEQUENCES OF *TORAH DILEI* – HALAKHIC AND OTHERWISE

The Teacher May Forgo His Honor

This interpretation in Avodah Zarah of the verse in Tehillim, that ultimately the Torah is the student's possession, is not merely a rhetorical flourish or an impassioned homily. It is the basis of a very important halakhah with far-reaching consequences. This halakhah is found in Kiddushin, which asks whether a father may forgo the *kavod*, the honor, which is due to him. The Gemara concludes that a father may forgo that which is due to him as a result of the commandment to "honor your father and mother." However, concerning the question of whether a teacher or a scholar may forgo the honor due to him, there is a dispute: R. Ḥisda says he may not, and R. Yosef says he may.[17]

For the moment, please note that the formulation "the teacher who waives the honor due to him" contains no qualifying adjective; the Gemara states simply, "the teacher," any teacher. We shall return to this soon in greater detail.

The scriptural proof that R. Yosef cites to sustain his position is the verse "The Lord went before them,"[18] which states that God came down, as it were, and led the way as the Children of Israel left Egypt. What greater forfeiture of honor is there than when God Himself accepts the task of leadership by walking before them, as it were?

Rava challenges R. Yosef's proof: How can one make an analogy like that? With respect to God, the world belongs to Him and the Torah

17. אמר רב חסדא: האב שמחל על כבודו, כבודו מחול, הרב שמחל על כבודו אין כבודו מחול; ורב יוסף אמר: אפילו הרב שמחל על כבודו, כבודו מחול שנאמר וַה׳ הֹלֵךְ לִפְנֵיהֶם יוֹמָם (שמות יג, כא; קידושין לב, א-ב).

18. וַה׳ הֹלֵךְ לִפְנֵיהֶם יוֹמָם. (שמות יג, כא)

belongs to Him; and thus He can forgo His own honor. But in the case of a scholar, how can we say that the Torah belongs to him, and that he can thus forgo his honor?[19] Rashi clarifies Rava's question: "The honor is that of the Torah, and the scholar has no right to forgo the Torah's honor, for it belongs to God."[20]

Rava then answers his own question:[21] The verse in Tehillim can be interpreted to mean that initially the Torah belongs to God, but once the scholar has invested himself in *talmud Torah* it becomes his.[22] This is the meaning we saw above at the beginning of the *shiur*, of "In his Torah does he meditate day and night." When the scholar realizes the ideal of investing time and effort in the study of Torah (*taraḥ bah*), when he commits himself to deep, insightful study of the Torah (*yehegeh*), then the Torah becomes his. And thus the teacher has the prerogative to forgo his honor, since the Torah's honor has become his honor.

We have so far established that Rava's interpretation in Avodah Zarah of the verse in Tehillim – that "*his* Torah" refers to the student of Torah and not to God – became the basis of a halakhah in Kiddushin. Rava, after answering his own question, supports R. Yosef's view that a teacher of Torah may forgo the honor due to him.

The Honor of Scholars and Kings

Another example of the application of *Torah dilei*, "*his* Torah," in a halakhic context emerges from the Gemara in Sanhedrin,[23] which tells the story of King Yanai, who came before the court of Shimon ben Shetaḥ. The latter wanted to show that he was not partial to or intimidated by the king, so he told Yanai to stand while testifying before the court like all witnesses are required to do; this is based on a biblical passage.

---

19. אמר רבא: הכי השתא, התם הקדוש ב"ה עלמא דיליה הוא ותורה דיליה היא, מחיל ליה ליקריה; הכא תורה דיליה היא?! (קידושין שם).

20. **הכא תורה דיליה היא:** בתמיהה – הכבוד תלוי בתורה ואינו יכול למחול על כבוד התורה שהיא של הקב"ה! (רש"י, קידושין לב, ב).

21. [כמו "הוא מותיב לה והוא מפרק לה". (פסחים נט, ב; בבא קמא מג, ב; סנהדרין נז, ב)]

22. הדר אמר רבא: אין, תורה דיליה היא! דכתיב, וּבְתוֹרָתוֹ יֶהְגֶּה יוֹמָם וָלָיְלָה. (קידושין לב, ב)

23. אתא [ינאי] ויתיב. אמר ליה שמעון בן שטח: ינאי המלך! עמוד על רגליך ויעידו בך. ולא לפנינו אתה עומד, אלא לפני מי שאמר והיה העולם אתה עומד, שנאמר וְעָמְדוּ שְׁנֵי הָאֲנָשִׁים אֲשֶׁר לָהֶם הָרִיב לִפְנֵי ה' (דברים יט, יז; סנהדרין יט, א).

Tosafot raise a question on that Gemara, but first we need to look at two texts which their question presupposes. The first is an account in the Gemara in Shevuot, where two Torah scholars appeared before the court of Ameimar and the latter allowed them both to sit while testifying. His reasoning was that the mitzvah of honoring Torah scholars[24] neutralized the opposing mitzvah requiring witnesses to stand in court.

The second source is the continuation of the Gemara in Kiddushin about who is permitted to forgo honor due to him. R. Ashi says: Even according to those (R. Yosef and Rava) who maintain that a *rav*, a Torah scholar, may forgo honor due to him, a king may certainly not do so.[25]

Against the background of these two sources, Tosafot in Sanhedrin, commenting on the story of King Yanai, ask why Yanai should have to stand if a scholar does not have to stand.[26] Doesn't R. Ashi's statement in Kiddushin imply that a king's honor is greater than that of a Torah scholar, and is therefore not subject to being waived?

Their answer brings us back to Rava's conception of *Torah dilei*, "his Torah." The king's honor is not personal but is rather a function of his office. R. Ashi derives this from the verse "You shall surely set a king over you"; the expression "over you" implies that "his fear should be upon you."[27] It is the office that demands a measure of respect and reverence, not the person of the king; that is the reason that he cannot forgo his honor. With regard to a scholar, however, we say *Torah dilei*, "his Torah"; he does have the prerogative to forgo his own honor or the honor of the Torah that he now possesses. This, answered Tosafot, indicates that the stature of a Torah scholar is, in fact, greater than that of a king. That is why Shimon ben Shetaḥ could demand of Yanai to stand, although Ameimar had permitted the two scholars before his court to

---

24. אֶת ה׳ אֱלֹקֶיךָ תִּירָא (דברים ו, יג; י, כ) לרבות תלמידי חכמים. (בבא קמא מא, ב)

25. אמר רב אשי: אפילו למאן דאמר הרב שמחל על כבודו, כבודו מחול, נשיא שמחל על כבודו אין כבודו מחול (קידושין לב, ב).

26. ואם תאמר, והא אמרינן התם אפילו תלמיד חכם אינו צריך לעמוד משום דהאי עשה והאי עשה, ועשה דכבוד תורה עדיף ... אבל ת״ח תורתו דיליה ויכול למחול היטב על כבודו דשלו היא (תוספות סנהדרין יט, א, ד״ה ינאי המלך עמוד).

27. שׂוֹם תָּשִׂים עָלֶיךָ מֶלֶךְ (דברים יז, טו) שתהא אימתו עליך. (קידושין לב, ב)

sit while testifying. Here then is another halakhic application of Rava's interpretation of *Torah dilei.*

The Scholar and the Principal Master

Let us now further clarify the meaning of *Torah dilei.* What does it mean that the Torah belongs to the human being who worked hard, applied himself, and reached great heights in his understanding of Torah? On the face of it, Rava's initial challenge to R. Yosef's proof was a cogent one as Rashi formulated it: "The honor is that of the Torah, and the scholar has no right to forgo the Torah's honor, for it belongs to God."

Thus, the question that needs to be answered is: In what way is it possible for the Torah to become the possession of the scholar who worked hard at mastering it? What are the practical consequences of this *kinyan,* this acquisition, of proprietary rights?[28] In what manner does ownership of the Torah manifest itself? Furthermore, is it possible that the obligations of this acquisition outweigh the rights, that the responsibilities outweigh the privileges?

In order to address these questions, let us look a bit more closely at the idea of *Torah dilei* and at the notion of forgoing one's own honor by virtue of the Torah being his possession.[29]

The Rambam in *Hilkhot Talmud Torah* sums up the conclusion of the halakhah of the Gemara as follows:

> If a principal master (*harav hamuvhak*) wishes to forgo his honor (*kevodo)* in all or one of the aforementioned matters,[30] for all

28. The word is used purposely. *Kinyan* is a very precise, technical word, which means acquiring proprietary rights in something. We will see that this is exactly what happens here. The *ḥakham* acquires proprietary rights – he makes a *kinyan* in the Torah. The last chapter at the end of *Pirkei Avot* is called *Perek Kinyan Torah,* the way in which you take possession of the Torah. The *baraita* tells us of the forty-eight ways in which we take possession of the Torah.
29. See n. 17 above and the text preceding the note.
30. "The aforementioned matters" refers back to halakhah 5, where the Rambam states: "A disciple is forbidden to refer to his master by name"; there must be distance between the teacher and the student. In halakhah 7 the Rambam says: "He is obligated to rise before his master as soon as he is visible to him in the distance," and not wait until he is four cubits away.

> or one of his disciples, he is authorized to do so. But even if he forgoes his honor, his disciple remains obligated to show him the respect (*lehadro*) due to all scholars – even when he forgoes that respect.[31]

Take note here that the Rambam emphasizes that even if he forgoes his honor (*kevodo*), his disciple remains obligated to show him respect (*lehadro*).

Earlier, when we saw the discussion in Kiddushin about whether a Torah scholar may forgo honor due to him, I drew attention to the fact that the noun *rav* had no qualifying adjective, and I want to return to this point. We have seen that the Rambam mentions something that is not mentioned in the talmudic source; namely, that *harav hamuvhak,* "a principal master or teacher," may forgo his honor. How did the Rambam draw the conclusion that this halakhah applies only to *harav hamuvhak*? What about a scholar who is not his principal master?

In fact, the *Kesef Mishneh* addresses this question and argues as follows. Since R. Yosef in Kiddushin derives his view that a scholar may forgo his honor from the fact that God Himself, as it were, led the Children of Israel out of Egypt, thereby waiving His own honor, and from this we learn that *even* one's principal master may choose to forgo his honor, then *kal vaḥomer,* a fortiori, any other scholar may certainly do so.[32]

However, another reading of the Rambam can lead one to the understanding that he seems to have limited in a radical way the Gemara which speaks of *harav* without a qualifying adjective. According to this alternate reading, the Rambam speaks specifically of *harav hamuvhak.*

---

31. הרב המובהק שרצה למחול על כבודו בכל הדברים האלו או באחד מהן לכל תלמידיו או לאחד מהן, הרשות בידו. ואף על פי שמחל, חייב התלמיד להדרו ואפילו בשעה שמחל. (**משנה תורה** הלכות תלמוד תורה ה, יא).

32. The position of the *Kesef Mishneh* is codified in his *Shulḥan Arukh*:

    "**וכולם** שמחלו על כבודם, כבודם מחול, ואעפ"כ מצוה לכבדם ולקום מפניהם קצת" (**שולחן ערוך יורה דעה** קמד, סעיף יד).

    When the *Shulḥan Arukh* states **וכולם** he implies both *rav muvhak,* as well as a *rav* who is not a *rav muvhak.*

In fact, the Brisker Rov, R. Velvel Soloveitchik, in his *Ḥiddushei Maran Riz Halevi*[33] says that when the Rambam wrote *harav hamuvhak* he meant *harav hamuvhak* exclusively, and thus he rejects the *kal vaḥomer* of the *Kesef Mishneh*. In order to understand this position, we need to clarify the respective halakhot of *kibbud* (honor) and *hiddur* (respect).

There is a distinction between *kibbud* and *hiddur*. As we just saw above with regard to *harav hamuvhak*, the Rambam's position is that even if he forgoes his honor, his disciple remains obligated to show him the respect (*lehadro*) due to all scholars. Take note that the Rambam refers in this halakhah to two distinct terms: *kavod*, honor, and *hiddur*, respect.

Concerning *hiddur*, the Rambam states at the beginning of chapter 6 of *Hilkhot Talmud Torah*:

> One is duty-bound to show respect (*lehadro*) to any disciple of the wise, even if he is not one's master; for it is said, "You shall rise up before the aged and show respect for the face of an elder (*zaken*), the latter being someone who has acquired (*kanah*) wisdom."[34]

One difference between *kibbud* and *hiddur* is that *kibbud* requires one to stand as a sign of respect for *harav hamuvhak*, while *hiddur* requires one to merely make a gesture of standing. The second difference is that as soon as you see *harav hamuvhak* approaching *kimlo einav*, from afar, you may not look away but must rather stand up immediately; by contrast, regarding other *talmidei ḥakhamim*, the requirement of *hiddur* is only at a distance of four cubits.

There is a close connection between *kibbud harav* and *kibbud av* (honoring one's father); the halakhah relates them to each other. The Rambam in the sixth chapter of *Hilkhot Mamrim* says that the requirement to stand before one's father is identical to the requirement to stand

---

33. הרב יצחק זאב סאלאווייציק, **חידושי מרן הרי"ז הלוי** על הרמב"ם, ירושלים תשמ"ח, דף א ע"א-ע"ב.

34. כל תלמיד חכמים מצוה להדרו ואף על פי שאינו רבו שנאמר מִפְּנֵי שֵׂיבָה תָּקוּם וְהָדַרְתָּ פְּנֵי זָקֵן (ויקרא יט, לב), זקן זה שקנה חכמה (**משנה תורה** הלכות תלמוד תורה ו, א).

before one's teacher.[35] Standing for one's teacher is the standard, the norm, and it defines the requirement to stand before one's father as well.

Returning to the distinction between *kibbud* and *hiddur,* on what basis does the Rambam require *hiddur* even after *kavod* has been waived? According to the Brisker Rov, they constitute two distinct halakhic categories. One is the honor (*kavod*) due to *harav hamuvhak,* which is comparable to the honor due to one's parents. The details of that are found in the fifth chapter of *Hilkhot Talmud Torah,* where the Rambam relates *kibbud harav* to *kibbud av*:

> Just as one is commanded to honor and revere his father, so is he obligated to honor and revere his master. Indeed, his obligation to his master is even greater than to his father.[36]

These halakhot of *kibbud,* of honoring, can all be waived by *harav hamuvhak,* whom the fifth chapter in *Hilkhot Talmud Torah* discusses; he can forgo the honor which is due to him as is the case with a father.

The second halakhah is that of *hiddur. Hiddur* is a gesture of respect for every *talmid ḥakham*; it is an expression of appreciation for anybody who has credentials of Torah. Anybody who represents Torah as a result of deep and persevering commitment and accomplishment deserves this *hiddur,* this gesture of respect and appreciation. It cannot be waived, and that is why if you look closely in the sixth chapter of *Hilkhot Talmud Torah,* which deals with scholars in general, as distinct from the fifth chapter, which deals with *harav hamuvhak,* there is no mention of forgoing. Forgoing is relevant only to the halakhot of *kavod* for *harav hamuvhak*; there is no forgoing *hiddur,* which is appropriate for scholars in general. That is the significance of the passage just cited: "One is duty-bound to show respect for any disciple of the wise, even if he is not one's master." [37] The reason that the Rambam provides is: "You shall rise up before the aged and show respect for the face of an elder [*zaken*],

35. ועומד מפניו (=מפני אביו) כדרך שהוא עומד מפני רבו. (**משנה תורה** הלכות ממרים ו, ג)

36. כשם שאדם מצווה בכבוד אביו ויראתו כך הוא חייב בכבוד רבו ויראתו יתר מאביו (**משנה תורה** הלכות תלמוד תורה ה, א).

37. See n. 34 above.

the latter being someone who has acquired [*kanah*] wisdom." Note the word *kanah* is taken literally to mean one who has acquired, as in the word *kinyan*, an acquisition;[38] he has made a *kinyan* in the Torah, he has acquired *ḥokhmah*, wisdom. This *hiddur*, this respect, cannot be waived.

On what is this difference based? What is the significance of this difference? It seems at first paradoxical that the honor that one owes his *rav hamuvhak* should be more easily waived than the gesture of respect that one owes other *ḥakhamim*.

The conclusion is clear. *Harav hamuvhak* discussed in the Rambam's fifth chapter may forgo what he earned by his teaching, that which is due to him as a result of his transmitting the *masorah*, that which he earned by his creative contributions to the understanding of Torah and by his direct relationship with students, with *talmidim* young and old, and particularly the young to whom he taught Torah, as we shall see below.[39] In other words, *kavod* for *harav hamuvhak* is what people owe him as a personal obligation, as an expression of gratitude. Were you not to express this gratitude you would be an ingrate. You benefit from somebody's learning, somebody who spent a lifetime in Torah and who then shares with you all his insights, novel interpretations, and new applications. You owe him something. This is the halakhah of forgoing one's personal *kavod*, which applies only to *harav hamuvhak*. But the scholar who has no personal relationship with me may not forgo the respect due to him because it is not his to forgo; it is God's.[40] This is *hiddur*, which unlike the *kavod* due *harav hamuvhak*, is directed toward the Torah itself. In the case of other scholars, the personal dimension is missing; there is only the objective relation to Torah, and those who represent it are the emissaries, as it were, of Torah.

There are many proofs that allow us to clarify this distinction between *talmidei ḥakhamim*, scholars of the Torah as a class, and *harav hamuvhak*, one's teacher with whom he has intensively studied.

The Gemara in Kiddushin (32b) says:

---

38. See n. 28 above.

39. See p. 55 below.

40. See n. 20 above.

> Rava served drinks at his son's wedding celebration; he poured a cup for R. Pappa and R. Huna son of R. Yehoshua, and they stood up before him.

R. Pappa and R. Huna showed some acknowledgment for their indebtedness to Rava. They did so even though from Rava's action it was clear that he had waived his own honor. It was as if he had said, "This is what I want to do, this is my way of expressing my joy, and the laws of *kavod* are suspended. Don't feel uncomfortable in letting me serve you." The Gemara continues:

> [However, when he poured a cup] for R. Mari and for R. Pinḥas son of R. Ḥisda, they did not stand up before him. [Rava] became angry and said: Are you sages, and the others not?[41]

Rashi explains: "You think that you are scholars and hence important, which is why you did not stand up before me; while your friends, those scholars who did stand up before me, are not scholars?"[42]

The discussion in the Gemara concludes that even if the scholar was willing to forgo his honor, others should have demonstrated *hiddur.*[43] Rashi explains the nature of this *hiddur:* "*Hiddur* means a voluntary gesture of beginning to rise."[44] *Meḥilah,* forgoing, applies only to *kavod;* but *hiddur,* the universal basis, the substratum, remains applicable to every scholar.

Although according to Rashi this *hiddur* is a voluntary gesture, the Rambam differs; he put this requirement for *hiddur* at the end of halakhah 11, as we saw above.

---

41. והא רבא משקי בי הלולא דבריה, ודל ליה כסא לרב פפא ולרב הונא בריה דרב יהושע וקמו מקמיה; לרב מרי ולרב פנחס בריה דרב חסדא, ולא קמו מקמיה. איקפד ואמר: הנו רבנן, רבנן; והנו רבנן לאו רבנן? (קידושין לב, ב).
42. **רבנן**: אתם חכמים וחשובים בעיניכם שלא עמדתם מפני, ורבנן חבריכם דקמו מפני לאו רבנן נינהו? ובלשון תימה אמר להם (רש"י, קידושין שם).
43. ותו, רב פפא הוה משקי בי הלולא דאבא מר בריה, ודלי ליה כסא לר' יצחק בריה דרב יהודה ולא קם מקמיה, ואיקפד! אפילו הכי, הידור מיעבד ליה בעו (קידושין שם).
44. **הידור**: לנוע מעט כאילו רוצה לעמוד מפניו. (רש"י שם)

> But even if he forgoes his honor, his disciple remains obligated to show him the respect (*lehadro*) due all scholars – even when he forgoes that respect.[45]

The Rambam derives this from his interpretation of the Gemara. Even after you have waived the *kavod*, the obligation of *hiddur*, which is a lesser one, remains. The reason for this is that *harav hamuvhak* is no less deserving than all other Torah scholars, and with respect to this group *hiddur* cannot be waived. This is evident from the language of the Rambam itself.[46] But even if he forgoes his *kavod*, his honor, his disciple remains obligated to show him the respect due all scholars: "One is duty-bound to show respect (*lehadro*) for any Torah scholar."[47]

I can tell you to forgo something that relates to me personally. I cannot tell you not to daven *ma'ariv* or not to do another mitzvah; that is something that is not in anybody's province. *Kavod* is an obligation of the student to *harav hamuvhak*; *hiddur* is a general obligation.

Rava had made it clear that he was not interested in *kavod*. According to Rashi, there was no residual obligation of *hiddur* either; it was just a voluntary gesture. According to the Rambam, however, *hiddur* remained obligatory. The Rambam is consistent in this distinction between *kavod* and *hiddur*. We see here the systematic unfolding in the Rambam's interpretation. *Kavod*, which arises from personal relationship, may be suspended; *hiddur* is an objective, impersonal obligation and therefore is always operative. *Hiddur* is not mine to forgo; it is a mitzvah, *mitzvah lehadro*, and therefore no one can exempt somebody else from doing a mitzvah.

Personal Humility and the Honor of the Torah

The well-known trait of great scholars to forgo the *kavod* that is due to them is reflected in the following passage of the Rambam.

---

45. See n. 31 above.

46. The Brisker Rov makes this point; see n. 33 above.

47. See n. 34 above.

> Though a scholar has the authority to invoke a ban in defense of his honor, it is not commendable for a disciple of the wise to conduct himself in this way. He ought rather to turn a deaf ear to the words of the ignorant.... This is the right path for disciples of the wise, which ought to be followed.[48]

There are many classic stories about how *ḥakhamim*, for significant causes, would expose themselves to humiliation in a manner which ordinary people would never consider.

But then the Rambam continues:

> But that is the case only if he was dishonored or reviled privately. If, however, a disciple of the wise was dishonored or reviled publicly, he is forbidden to forgive the affront to his honor. And if he does, he will be called to account; for that would constitute dishonor of the Torah.[49]

To illustrate: You come to somebody and ask him to contribute toward the Torah education institution you are building – I remember how many times the Rov used to do this in the early years, asking for a contribution to Maimonides School – and not only does he show disrespect, but he rejects you and what you stand for. You begin to silently walk away; however, you stop, you persist, ultimately receive the contribution and leave, completely overlooking the contemptuous humiliation. This is what the Rambam says about this trait of scholars, that they would never invoke a ban as a punishment that was theirs to invoke if something was not public.

However, if this was done publicly he has no right to forgo his *kavod*, and if he does, he is punished, for it is not his *kavod*. Rashi already addressed this: "The honor is that of the Torah and not of the scholar;

48. אף על פי שיש רשות לחכם לנדות לכבודו, אינו שבח לתלמיד חכם להנהיג עצמו בדבר זה; אלא מעלים אזניו מדברי עם הארץ... וזו היא דרכם של תלמידי חכמים שראוי לילך בה... (**משנה תורה** הלכות תלמוד תורה ז, יג).

49. במה דברים אמורים? כשבזהו או חרפהו בסתר. אבל תלמיד חכם שבזהו או חרפו אדם בפרהסיא – אסור לו למחול על כבודו; ואם מחל – נענש, שזה בזיון תורה (שם).

that honor belongs to God,"[50] and nobody has the right to forgo it, not even *harav hamuvhak*!

Another manifestation of humility is expressed in the Gemara in Kiddushin:

> From where is it derived that an elder should not trouble others [to honor him]?[51]

The elder, *zaken,* which is interpreted to mean *zeh shekanah ḥokhmah,* he who has acquired wisdom, a scholar to whom you are obligated to show *hiddur,* is forbidden to needlessly cause you to show respect. Rashi explains:

> He should not trouble others if it is possible for him to take a different path, and thereby avoid requiring the public to stand [in his honor].[52]

The Rambam quotes this in *Hilkhot Talmud Torah.*[53] If a scholar for whom people would stand, or at least make a gesture, can come in from the side, he should do so rather than wait until everyone is seated and walk down the middle so that everybody will be disrupted. That is the meaning of "an elder should not trouble others." The Gemara says that this is based on the verse "And you shall revere the face of an elder, and you shall fear your God."[54] This last clause is usually applied to the people who are obligated to show *kavod*. However, the Gemara here applies it to the *zaken*, to the elder, who is receiving the honor. If you, the *zaken*, know that there is no need to disrupt people and you needlessly create such a circumstance, you have violated "You shall fear your God."

---

50. See n. 20 above.

51. מנין לזקן שלא יטריח? (קידושין לב, ב)

52. **שלא יטריח:** אם יכול לילך דרך אחרת שלא יעמיד את הציבור. (רש"י שם)

53. אין ראוי לחכם שיטריח את העם ויכוין עצמו להן כדי שיעמדו מפניו, אלא ילך בדרך קצרה ומתכוין שלא יראה אותו אחד, כדי שלא יטריחו לעמוד (**משנה תורה** הלכות תלמוד תורה ו, ג; והשווה הלכות סנהדרין כה, ב).

54. מנין לזקן שלא יטריח? ת"ל [מִפְּנֵי שֵׂיבָה תָּקוּם וְהָדַרְתָּ פְּנֵי] **זָקֵן וְיָרֵאתָ** [מֵּאֱלֹקֶיךָ] (ויקרא יט, לב; קידושין לב, ב).

Here too you might ask: Why is this? If the elder, *zeh shekanah ḥokhmah,* who is wise, has proprietary rights to the Torah by virtue of *Torah dilei,* why shouldn't he be able to trouble people, to create even artificially a situation where they have to stand to show respect for him? The answer is that the motive counts; the circumstances count. If the setting is artificial, and, as Rashi emphasizes, "If it is possible for him to take a different path and thereby avoid requiring the public to stand in his honor," then the focus is no longer *kevod hatorah* but my own honor, my own ego. That is how the Gemara interprets *veyareita me'Elokekha,* "and you shall fear your God"; every person, including the scholar, has to take into account that God can read his intentions and knows his motives.

In short, you see from this last particularly significant halakhah that the halakhot of the honor due to a scholar are always related, both positively and negatively, to the honor of the Torah, to that aspect of honor which may never be forfeited. If *Torah dilei* is not manifesting itself in a natural, harmonious way, there should be no obligation to show respect because of the artificiality of the situation.

Until now we saw the interpretation of the Gemara in Avodah Zarah of *uvetorato yehegeh,* "in his Torah does he meditate," as referring to the scholar's own Torah, *Torah dilei.* Then we saw how the Gemara in Kiddushin applies this in firm halakhic terms to the question of the scholar forgoing his honor. Since it is the scholar's Torah, he may waive his honor. I mentioned the Tosafot in Sanhedrin that quotes these words, *Torah dilei,* his Torah, in explaining the difference between a scholar and a king; the king's honor stems from his office whereas the scholar's honor stems from the Torah that he has acquired. We then saw the distinction between *harav hamuvhak* and all other scholars according to the Rambam. These are all consequences of *Torah dilei.* But how does *Torah dilei* express itself in the way the Torah scholar studies and understands Torah?

The Identification of the Scholar with his Torah

We have seen that *Torah dilei* means that the Torah is his because of his exemplary dedication to study and his powers of creativity. As a result, authority is vested in him to determine the interpretation and the application of the Torah. Torah scholars use traditional categories of analysis and are able to develop new insights, new conceptualizations.[55] God bequeathed this right to them. This is the essence of *Torah dilei*; that is its precise meaning as we saw in the Gemara in Avodah Zarah, where Rava said:

> Initially the Torah is called by the name of the Holy One, blessed be He, but ultimately it is called by the name of the one who studies it.[56]

"It is called by the name of the one who studies it," quite literally. We speak of the ordinances of Rabban Yoḥanan ben Zakkai, of the halakhot of R. Akiva, of the judicial decisions of the Rambam and of the *Meḥaber*, R. Yosef Karo; these are all "called by his name." We speak of the interpretations of the *Noda Beyehudah* and R. Akiva Eiger not as anonymous Torah but as the Torah of the *Noda Beyehudah*, of R. Akiva Eiger; this is what we mean when we speak of the Torah of the Rov. These are all examples of "called by his name."

A further extension of this principle is that *Torah dilei* underlies the halakhah that the Torah is *lo bashamayim hi*, "is not in heaven";[57] it is interpreted and applied only by *talmidei ḥakhamim* and not by supernatural intervention.

OBLIGATIONS IMPOSED BY *TORAH DILEI*

We have seen that the concept of *Torah Dilei* confers prerogatives and authority upon the scholar who has earned them by his dedication and creativity. This special status also entails obligations rooted in spiritual, intellectual, and moral integrity. I want to now identify a few of them.

When to Teach and When to Refrain

Spiritual and intellectual integrity are among the fundamental characteristics of a Torah scholar. This is well illustrated by the Rambam in *Hilkhot Talmud Torah*:

---

55. See the discussion of *ḥiddush*, pp. 134 ff.

56. See n. 2 above.

57. Devarim 30:12, as interpreted in Bava Metzia 59b.

> A disciple who has not attained to competence but rules nonetheless, is daft, wicked, and arrogant. Of him it was said: "For many are those she has struck dead" (Mishlei 7:26).

A person who inflates his own importance is not worthy to be a leader and to issue a halakhic decision. The verse that the Rambam cites adds that such Torah is not only unworthy but is destructive as well. This is the negative side of spiritual, intellectual integrity. On the other hand, continues the Rambam, one who is qualified is not allowed to shirk responsibility, because he who does that is in the category of one who "withholds Torah":

> By the same token, a scholar who *has* attained to competence in ruling but does not rule, withholds Torah, and sets stumbling blocks before the blind. Of him it was said: "And numerous are her victims" (ibid.).[58]

There are corpses either way: when an unworthy, unqualified person comes to the fore, then "many are those she has struck dead"; when a worthy, qualified person does *not* come forward, then "numerous are her victims."

The Rambam discusses both here and in *Hilkhot Sanhedrin*[59] this inner struggle of the scholar. A true scholar does not want to be in the limelight. The Torah shuns publicity; it is a *kli tzanu'a,* unpretentious,[60] and those who are associated with it, who are emissaries of Torah, share the same trait. Nevertheless, they may not shirk responsibility to teach

58. וכל תלמיד שלא הגיע להוראה ומורה – הרי זה שוטה, רשע וגס הרוח, ועליו נאמר: כִּי רַבִּים חֲלָלִים הִפִּילָה. וכן חכם שהגיע להוראה ואינו מורה – הרי זה מונע תורה, ונותן מכשולות לפני העיוורים, ועליו נאמר וַעֲצֻמִים כָּל הֲרֻגֶיהָ (משלי ז, כו; **משנה תורה** הלכות תלמוד תורה ה, ד). המונח "מונע תורה" שאב הרמב"ם מהגמרא הזאת: כל **המונע** הלכה מפי תלמיד כאילו גזלו מנחלת אבותיו (סנהדרין צא, ב).

59. כך היה דרך חכמים הראשונים: בורחין מלהתמנות, ודוחקין עצמן הרבה שלא ישבו בדין עד שידעו שאין שם ראוי כמותם, ושאם ימנעו מן הדין תקלקל השורה; אעפ"כ לא היו יושבין בדין אלא עד שמכבידין עליהם העם והזקנים ופוצרים בם (**משנה תורה** הלכות סנהדרין ג, י).

60. See pp. 23 ff.

Torah. There is a delicate balance, and one may imperceptibly cross the line; this requires a high degree of sensitivity and self-examination.

Another illustration of the need for spiritual and intellectual integrity is the following striking halakhah in *Hilkhot Sanhedrin*:

> A judge who is presented with a legal question, and begins by comparing the legal question to an existing codified law (*din pasuk*) with which he is familiar – if there is a greater scholar in his city, and he does not consult with him, he is considered as one of the sinners who cavalierly makes judicial decisions.[61]

This is a powerful statement. On the one hand you are knowledgeable in Halakhah. You are capable of examining the case and you compare it with previously adjudicated law which seems to be identical to the case before you. It is a *din pasuk*, clearly decided, and you are sure of yourself. But you have an opportunity to deepen your knowledge, to inquire further, for there is a greater scholar near you with whom you can consult. If you do not consult with him then you, the scholar, become a sinner. What a metamorphosis, what a transformation, from a *dayan* who is speaking on behalf of Torah to a sinner!

Teaching Torah to the Young

The Gemara in Kiddushin says:

> R. Ḥiyya bar Abba encountered R. Yehoshua ben Levi, who had thrown a covering on his head and brought his child to the synagogue to study. R. Ḥiyya bar Abba said to him: What is happening here? R. Yehoshua ben Levi said to him: Is what is written insignificant: "Make them known to your sons," juxtaposed to "The day when you stood before the Lord your God in Ḥoreb"?[62]

61. כל דיין שבא לפניו דין והתחיל לדמותו לדין פסוק שכבר ידע אמתו, ויש במדינה גדול ממנו בחכמה, ואינו הולך ונמלך בו – הרי זה בכלל הרשעים שלבם גס בהוראה (**משנה תורה** הלכות סנהדרין כ, ח).

62. רבי חייא בר אבא אשכחיה לריב"ל, דשדי דיסנא ארישיה וקא ממטי ליה לינוקא לבי כנישתא; א"ל: מאי כולי האי? א"ל: מי זוטר מאי דכתיב וְהוֹדַעְתָּם לְבָנֶיךָ, וסמיך ליה יוֹם אֲשֶׁר עָמַדְתָּ

R. Ḥiyya b. Abba could not understand what this great sage R. Yehoshua b. Levi was doing rushing to bring his son to the synagogue; had he nothing more important to do? He said to R. Yehoshua b. Levi: Isn't it a bit much? R. Yehoshua b. Levi replied: Is it insignificant that the Torah characterizes one who transmits Torah to children as one who is standing at Mount Sinai? The Gemara reports that after this encounter, R. Ḥiyya would not eat breakfast until he had the opportunity to review with his son what he had learned the day before and to add something. Only then would he eat breakfast. Thus, *torah dilei* entails not only rights and prerogatives but, more importantly, responsibilities and duties.

Moral and Intellectual Integrity in Writing *Ḥiddushei Torah*

There is a responsum of the Netziv[63] concerning whether one has the right to destroy his own writings of *divrei Torah*. Someone's father, a great *rav*, had instructed his son to destroy all the responsa he had written, because he felt that they were inferior to his *ḥiddushei Torah*, his Torah novellae. The son asked the Netziv whether he is obligated to fulfill his father's directive. The Netziv takes the position that responsa can be more significant than *ḥiddushei Torah*. He then suggests that one might have thought, based on the Gemara in Avodah Zarah that we saw, that one acquires ownership, has proprietary rights to the Torah, and therefore he can do what he wants, even destroy it. The Netziv rejects that claim. The ownership of a scholar over his Torah is like that of one who is giving his *terumah* to a *kohen*; he can choose the recipient *kohen*, but he may not destroy the *terumah*.

And yet there are examples of *gedolei Torah* who did destroy their Torah. Perhaps the most famous is the author of *Ḥiddushei Harim*, the first Gerer Rebbe. Notwithstanding his many *sefarim* on the Torah, *Shas*, and *Rishonim* that we study all the time, we have testimony of his grandson, a brother of the Sfat Emet, who saw him burning some of his *sefarim*. "Why are you doing that?" he asked his grandfather. The Ḥiddushei Harim explained to him that even *ḥiddushei Torah* have to

---

לִפְנֵי ה׳ אֱלֹקֶיךָ בְּחֹרֵב? מכאן ואילך, רבי חייא בר אבא לא טעים אומצא, עד דמקרי לינוקא ומוספיה (קידושין ל, א).

63. **משיב דבר** א, ד

be written for the honor of the Holy One, blessed be He. Any doubt whether your motives were pure vitiates the Torah you have written. He was selecting those which he did not think deserved to endure. We also know of another *sefer* that he had written that his teacher, the Kotzker Rebbe, told him would replace the *Siftei Kohen,* an authoritative commentary to the *Shulḥan Arukh,* which would be improper. That was all the Kotzker Rebbe said to him, and he burnt that *sefer.*

Lest you think that this was characteristic only of the great ḥasidic leaders, the Sha'agat Aryeh states at the beginning of his *sefer* that he carefully identified what he thought was *pilpul,* that he did not want to endure. "Let the wind carry them away," he said. What we have in our editions of the *Sha'agat Aryeh* are his classic monumental investigations into themes of Torah that in his opinion were based on the proper method.

Moral Qualities When Studying Torah

There are many ethical traits which are prerequisites for the acquisition and retention of Torah. As I mentioned earlier, it is not accidental that the sixth chapter in *Pirkei Avot* is called *Perek Kinyan Torah,* "the ways in which the Torah is acquired." If you aspire to acquire Torah you must cultivate moral traits to a high degree of perfection. The lack of these traits, regardless of your intellectual achievements, vitiates and diminishes the Torah and calls into question not only one's acquisition but one's very relation to Torah. This moral impeccability is expressed even in the context of *pilpulah shel Torah,* the give and take of halakhic analysis.

The Gemara in Menaḥot tells us of the difference between the bringing of the *omer* on Pesaḥ and the *shtei haleḥem* on Shavuot. The Gemara describes a debate in which R. Tarfon was puzzled about the difference between the *omer* and the *shtei haleḥem.* A young scholar, R. Yehudah son of Neḥemiah, explained to him the difference. R. Tarfon was silent, acknowledging thereby that R. Yehudah son of Neḥemiah had explained the halakhah properly.

The Gemara then tells us that R. Yehudah son of Neḥemiah was filled with self-satisfaction and pleasure that he had bested the senior scholar. R. Akiva said to the young scholar, "Your face shows your great satisfaction and pleasure; your cheeks are filled with extra color after you rebutted the elder scholar." R. Akiva then concluded, "I doubt very much if you have a long life in store for you." [64]

This is an example of the high moral standards to which Torah scholars who have earned the status of possessing *Torah dilei* are held.

Actually the first instance of what we started with, of *uvetorato yehegeh,* he will meditate upon *his* Torah, of *Torah hanikreit al shemo,* Torah that is now attributed to him (to the scholar), is recorded in the Gemara Shabbat regarding Moshe Rabbeinu. I mention it because it shows the inseparability between the intellectual and moral virtues. The Gemara tells us that after Moshe Rabbeinu received the Torah, the *Satan* came in pursuit of it. After not finding it anywhere, he finally asked Moshe Rabbeinu if he had the Torah. Moshe Rabbeinu responded, "Who am I? Am I sufficiently worthy for God to have given *me* the Torah?" The Holy One, blessed be He, said to Moshe: "Are you a liar?" Did you deny to the *Satan* that indeed I gave you the Torah? Moshe answered that he simply could not make such a claim.[65] "Will I be self-congratulatory and say, 'Yes, I am the great person who deserved to take this treasure that would delight God every day'?"

The Gemara then concludes that God said to Moshe, "Since you have shown such humility, the Torah will be known by your name. The *navi* will say, 'Be mindful of the Torah of My servant Moshe.'" [66] This is the first instance of Torah being *nikreit al shemo,* of Torah being attributed to a person. But note that this instance of *nikreit al shemo* is not for his intellectual attainment, not because "no prophet again rose in

64. יתיב רבי טרפון וקא קשיא ליה: מה בין קודם לעומר לקודם שתי הלחם? אמר לפניו יהודה בר נחמיה: לא, אם אמרת קודם לעומר שכן לא הותר מכללו אצל הדיוט, תאמר קודם לשתי הלחם שהותר מכללו אצל הדיוט? שתק רבי טרפון. צהבו פניו של רבי יהודה בן נחמיה. אמר לו רבי עקיבא: יהודה, צהבו פניך שהשבת את זקן, תמהני אם תאריך ימים (מנחות סח, ב).

65. This is in accord with the halakhot in Bava Metzia (23b–24a) about when a scholar is allowed to deviate from the truth.

66. וא"ר יהושע בן לוי: בשעה שירד משה מלפני הקב"ה בא שטן ואמר לפניו: רבונו של עולם, תורה היכן היא? אמר לו... אמר לו: לך אצל בן עמרם. הלך אצל משה אמר לו: תורה שנתן לך הקב"ה היכן הוא? אמר לו: וכי מה אני שנתן לי הקדוש ברוך הוא תורה? אמר לו הקדוש ברוך הוא למשה: משה, בדאי אתה? אמר לפניו: רבונו של עולם, חמודה גנוזה יש לך שאתה משתעשע בה בכל יום; אני אחזיק טובה לעצמי? אמר לו הקדוש ברוך הוא למשה: הואיל ומיעטת עצמך – תקרא על שמך, שנאמר זִכְרוּ תּוֹרַת מֹשֶׁה עַבְדִּי וגו'. (מלאכי ג, כב; שבת פט, א).

Israel like Moshe."[67] It is rather because of Moshe's moral virtue, which sustains and supports his intellectual virtue.

* * *

In this *shiur,* I have not talked much about the Rov. But it is self-evident that anything that one says in *divrei Torah* reflects the Rov's Torah. His Torah and his example – and I say very carefully *both* his Torah and his example – underlie the halakhah of *Torah dilei,* the theme of this *shiur.* Would that we could still hear the Rov's Torah, would that each of us were able to ask one more question, to hear some insight from the Rov, just to remind ourselves what we had, what we have in his Torah, and what we are missing in his person.

יהי זכרו ברוך

67. וְלֹא קָם נָבִיא עוֹד בְּיִשְׂרָאֵל כְּמֹשֶׁה. (דברים לד, י)

חכמים ותלמידיהם

Chapter 3

The Sages and Their Students

TEACHERS AND THEIR STUDENTS: RECIPROCITY AND MUTUALITY[1]

The phrase *ḥakhamim vetalmideihem,* the Sages and their students, is found in the *Sifrei* and was given prominence by the Rambam, who uses

1. [Rabbi Twersky opened this *shiur* with the following direct address to the audience: The life of the Rov, who so shunned artificiality and pompousness, vacuous ceremonialism and officiousness, was a dramatic representation of the story of *ḥakhamim vetalmideihem*. He was certainly our generation's most distinguished and most brilliant member of this *ḥavurah,* this small but vital group – the *ḥakham hamasorah*, the sage of tradition, par excellence. Those influenced by the Rov's teachings – those whose spiritual existence was enhanced and enriched, whose understanding of Torah was deepened by his inspirational directives, and whose commitment to a meticulous observance of mitzvot was fortified by his inspirational guidance, by his profound insights and novel perspectives – should be especially mindful that rigorous honesty, free of hyperbole, free of any stream-of-consciousness association, is required not only in talking about the accomplishments and influence of the Rov, but also in describing our relationship to him. We should not easily or indiscriminately, without accountability

it twice in *Hilkhot De'ot*.[2] *Ḥakhamim vetalmideihem* will provide us with a key to understanding the special *masorah* community of teaching and studying which the Rov described in his *hesped* for my mother, the Rebbetzin, *aleha hashalom*, as the society "which was founded by Moshe at the dawn of our history and which at the point of eschatological fulfillment of our history will be joined by the King Messiah."[3]

[We must ask: Who is a genuine student of a *ḥakham*? What is the nature of discipleship? What are the qualities of mind and soul that a student must possess to be considered a student of the wise?]

It would be helpful to recall the moving words, in their forceful and eloquent simplicity, of Reb Ḥayyim Volozhiner, who by consensus of his contemporaries and followers was the outstanding disciple of the Gra, the Vilna Gaon. A fellow disciple of the Gaon, R. Yisrael Mishklov, in his *Taklin Ḥaditin* said about Reb Ḥayyim: "He saw the sun in all its intensity." Reb Ḥayyim himself proclaimed with such compelling candor that he did not deserve to be referred to as a *talmid* of the Gra. This Reb Ḥayyim was the visionary founder of the Yeshiva of Volozhin and, as a result, the prime architect of the yeshiva movement of the last two centuries, as well as the inspired formulator of an authoritative, carefully crafted, and highly influential ideology of Torah study. I think it would be hard to find many works that were as influential, as epochal, as decisive as the *Nefesh Haḥayyim*. Reb Ḥayyim, in his genuine modesty and overpowering reverence for his rebbe, wrote as follows in a letter at the time of the founding of the Volozhiner Yeshiva:

> I have heard that my name has been associated with our teacher, who is known to be so great throughout the Jewish diaspora that his very name is recognized as greater than any title of honor that can be accorded to him; our master and teacher, Israel's holy one, its beacon of light, the Gaon our master R. Eliyahu, whose soul is

---

for our words, claim the honorific title "*talmid* of the Rov." This is high praise indeed, and could conveniently be self-serving and self-congratulatory instead of being a catalyst for more study and enhanced observance.]

2. *Sifrei, Devarim, Eikev* 49; *Mishneh Torah, Hilkhot De'ot* 6:2.
3. See "A Tribute to the Rebbetzin of Talne," *Tradition* 17:2 (1978), 75.

> in heaven, the devoutly pious one of Vilna. I have had the honor of being identified as his student, thus associating me with his worthy name. I hereby see it as my duty to sincerely declare that Heaven forbid that I blemish the honor of the great and sacred Rabbi, whose soul is in heaven, by being identified with him.
>
> Anyone who says that is, I declare with total honesty, completely in error. The Gaon, whose soul is in heaven, mastered the entire corpus of Torah with systematic clarity, resulting in clearly formulated halakhah without any uncertainties. He possessed encyclopedic knowledge of the written Torah, the Mishnah, the Babylonian and the Jerusalem Talmuds, the *Mekhilta, Sifra, Sifrei, Tosefta,* all the Midrashim, all sections of the *Zohar,* and every statement made by every *tanna* and every *amora.* He had total knowledge of them all, and he was able to resolve all difficulties that arose in the study of those texts. Furthermore, he developed new insights into all of these sources by listening to their nuances, and by drawing upon vast numbers of halakhot, aggadot, and sources from esoteric literature.
>
> How then can I be so presumptuous and not be mortified to be called his student when I have not succeeded in absorbing even the most meager portion of his splendor?[4]

Pay attention to the symmetry in the way Reb Ḥayyim is expressing this idea: that by people calling him a *talmid* of the Gra, they are associating the Gra with him, and vice versa. And it is this association which is a matter of such great import and such great seriousness for Reb Ḥayyim

---

4. ואנכי שמעתי, שנקרא עלי שם רבנו הגדול מרבן שמו בכל תפוצות ישראל מרנא ורבנא קדוש ישראל ואורו הגאון מוהר"ר אליהו נ"ע חסיד מווילנא. וזכיתי להקרא בשמו הטוב עלי לאמר שאני תלמידו. וראיתי החובה לעצמי ולהודיע בישראל נאמנה, שחלילה לי לפגום בכבוד הרב רבנו הגדול והקדוש נ"ע להקרא שמי עליו. וידעתי נאמנה שכל האומר כן אינו אלא טועה גמור, כי הגאון נ"ע משנתו סדורה להלכה ברורה בכל התורה כולה בלא שום ספיקא, גמיר במקרא במשנה, בש"ס בבלי וירושלמי, ומכילתא ספרא וספרי ותוספתא, מדרשים וזוהרים וכל דברי תנאים ואמוראים הנמצאים בכולם זכה להיות חלקו בהם. והכריע בין הספיקות המתילדים בדבריהם, ולחדש בהם דברים להיות שומע ומוסיף בהם תלי תלים של הלכות ואגדות ורזי דרזין. ואיך אשים פני כחלמיש ולא אבוש להקרא בשם תלמידו אחר שלא זכיתי לקבל מהודו אפילו מקצת (מכתב מרבנו ר' חיים מוולוז'ין זי"ע, **הפלס** ב', טבת תרס"ב, עמ' 142).

Volozhiner. "Anyone who says that is, I declare with total honesty, completely in error."

The term *talmid* suggests reciprocity, some mutuality between *rav* and *talmid*; and even allowing for the absolute superiority of the teacher, the very reciprocity can be demeaning. Accepting this description of himself as *talmid harav* without any qualification would demean the Gra's honor. "Heaven forbid that I blemish the honor of the great and sacred Rabbi, whose soul is in heaven, by being identified with him."

He then goes on to characterize the Gra, a characterization that will make clear the gap between the *talmid* and the rebbe:

> He possessed encyclopedic knowledge of the written Torah, the Mishnah, the Babylonian and the Jerusalem Talmuds, the *Mekhilta, Sifra, Sifrei, Tosefta,* all the Midrashim, all sections of the *Zohar,* and every statement made by every *tanna* and every *amora.*

And he concludes: "How then can I be so presumptuous and not be mortified to be called his student?"

Concerning our relationship with the Rov, it is clear that one must use the phrase "*talmid* of the Rov" carefully and honestly, responsibly and sensitively, with a measure of restraint and respect. But more significantly, we who try to be his *talmidim,* to confront the profundity and originality as well as the delicacy and dynamism of his Torah, to appreciate his great intuition, to bask in the warmth and light of his genius, we should persist in our efforts to understand and appropriate his Torah, to engage in meditation and reflection, to the extent that this meditation is galvanized by a moral-spiritual teleology, with a clear purpose – *nisht stam in der velt* – not aimlessly.

We need to be attentive to his teaching and to his behavior. This is the authentic living *masorah* which we have. I said, "We should persist in our efforts" for a simple reason: Understanding a *ḥakham,* a rebbe, is an ongoing, open-ended process. It is not something that came to an end with the Rov's passing[5] or a few years earlier during the long

5. [The Rov passed away on 18 Nissan 5753 (1993).]

sickness of the Rov, when our privilege to hear him was no longer possible. Understanding a *ḥakham* is an ongoing process, both cognitively and experientially, and is not contained temporally.

The task of the *ḥakham* as opposed to that of the *talmid* is simple: he transmits Torah, he shares his vast erudition and uncanny insights, thereby perpetuating and enhancing the *masorah*. The Gra states:

> In every generation a spark of Moshe Rabbeinu lights the way for a unique soul of the generation. He, in turn, enlightens the entire generation.[6]

This sounds like the Mezritcher Maggid; it sounds like the Ba'al Hatanya; but this was written by none other than the Gra. What is striking about this sentence in which each word is so carefully measured is that the function of this spark coming from Moshe Rabbeinu is first to illuminate the unique *ḥakham* of the generation, and then in turn, through him, to illuminate the generation.

THE TASK OF STUDENTS

The task of students is an ongoing one. The initial contact and exposure require sustained reflection. In commenting on the Gemara in Berakhot, "The merit of attending a lecture lies in the running,"[7] Rashi introduces a subtle, critical distinction between *agra depirka*, the merit of attending a lecture that *Ḥazal* are referring to, and the reward for retaining the understanding of the *sevara*, the logical analysis of the halakhah. Rashi explains:

> The primary reward for those who run to hear a *derashah* from a *ḥakham* is the reward for the running, since most of them do not retain the understanding of the teaching, and cannot repeat

---

6. בכל דור ודור ניצוץ אחד ממשה רבנו ע"ה מאיר לחד בדור והוא מאיר לכל בני דורו (הגר"א, **יהל אור**, וילנא תרמ"ב, השמטות סוף ספר בראשית דף ל ע"ב).

7. אגרא דפרקא רְהטא. (ברכות ו, ב)

> what they heard from their teacher afterward – by which they would earn reward for their study.[8]

This is a remarkable statement. Rashi is not saying that those who are running to hear do not understand the *shiur.* We give them the benefit of the doubt. What Rashi is saying is that earning the reward for *limmud,* for the study of Torah, entails not only being physically present in a *shiur* or the ability to follow the analysis and understand the intricacies at the time they are being presented, but the ability to reproduce accurately at a later time that which the rebbe had said. One must retain or retrieve all its vitality and pungency without any distortion or deflection or dulling of the novel ideas and nuances heard in the *shiur,* and not allow time to impinge on the content, context, or contours of the halakhah. The reward for study according to Rashi is predicated upon achieving the status of a loyal *talmid,* and this status, discipleship, is open-ended – maintained and expressed even posthumously. The *talmid* is not free to engage in self-mirroring but is obligated to retain the teaching, and to repeat what he heard from his teacher precisely, *l'aḥar zman,* long afterward. He must take great pains to reproduce what he learned with unfailing accuracy, to be certain of any citation or attribution. This is where *talmidim,* perhaps, have to become something else; they need to become *yoshvim lifnei ḥakhamim,*[9] those who sit before the wise, as explained by Reb Ḥayyim Volozhiner in his commentary to Avot, *Ru'aḥ Ḥayyim.* It means to have a discerning, discriminating sense, nurtured by knowledge and intuition, so as to be able to understand the correct core teaching, and not to be confused by experimental formulations tentatively put forward and subsequently dropped. Thus, says Reb Ḥayyim:

> (This student) thinks in a discerning way. He knows how to uncover straightforward, authentic interpretations... it is well known that in the process of studying the Halakhah, explanations

---

8. **אגרא דפרקא:** עיקר קבול שכר הבריות הרצים לשמוע דרשה מפי חכם היא שכר המרוצה, שהרי רובם אינם מבינים להעמיד גירסא ולומר שמועה מפי רבם לאחר זמן, שיקבלו שכר לימוד (רש"י, ברכות שם).

9. Avot 5:15.

> that are incorrect arise, and only after insightful analysis, does God, may He be blessed, come to his aid and enlighten him so that he comprehends the truth.[10]

The analytic process of study must be followed, but *halakhah berurah*, the clearly formulated halakhah, which itself reflects a *mishnah sedurah*, a mastery of Torah with systematic clarity,[11] is what the *yosheiv lifnei ḥakhamim*, the student with a discerning, discriminating sense, nurtured by knowledge and intuition should be able to grasp.

One must also be loyal to the original setting of Torah, to be careful not to blur its uniqueness by utilizing categories and concepts that are foreign to Torah. The Rov writes in his *hesped* for his uncle, the Brisker Rov:

> The *lamdanut*, the scholarship, of his [Reb Ḥayyim of Brisk's] *beit midrash* must be authentic and original, stamped with the noetic creativity of the thinker.... The introduction of stereotyped logical arguments, reusing the stock formulations of other scholars, repeating ideas and Torah insights which hover in the air and are known by every yeshiva student, wrapping himself in a tallit which is not his own... gathering scattered opinions from the world of learning like the leaves that fall on a clear fall day in a thick forest... all these are foreign to the creative and authentic methodology of Reb Ḥayyim.[12]

10. [משמרת, שמוציאה את היין וקולטת את השמרים] שיש לו שכל ישר שהוא מברר הפשטים האמיתים ... כי ידוע כשלומדים בעיון הלכה, בתחלה לפעמים, עולים כמה סברות שאינם אמיתים, עד שאחר העיון השם יתברך מסייעו ומאיר עיניו לבוא אל האמת. (ר׳ חיים מוולוז׳ין, **רוח חיים** על מסכת אבות ירושלים תשנ״ד, ה, טו, עמ׳ קמו).

11. See n. 4 above for the description by Reb Ḥayyim of Volozhin of the Gra's comprehensive and creative methodology.

12. English translation adapted from Jeffrey Saks, "Rabbi Joseph B. Soloveitchik on the Brisker Method," *Tradition* 33:2 (1999), 53–54.
הלמדנות של בית מדרש זה צריכה להיות אותנטית, מקורית, טבועה בחותם היצירה הנואיטית של ההוגה ... הכנסת שיקולים הגיוניים שאולים, שימוש במטבעות שיצקו חכמי ישראל אחרים, חזרה על רעיונות וחידושי תורה המרחפים באוויר שכל בן ישיבה ידע אותם, התעטפות בטלית שאינה שלו... קיבוץ סברות מפוזרות בעולם הלומדים כשלכת עלים ביום סתיו ביער עבות

This is what in Yiddish used to be called *skarboveh torah,* trite or banal "torah," and that is what the Rov says was rejected in the Brisker tradition. This is part of what is required from a *talmid* who sits before the wise.

There is a story about R. Ya'akov Yosef of Polnoye, the author of the *Toldot Ya'akov Yosef,* the first printed work of Ḥasidut, who quotes close to three hundred *ma'amarim,* three hundred *divrei Torah,* in the name of the Ba'al Shem Tov. These sayings are often introduced by the phrase *shamati mimori,* "I have heard from my teacher." On a few occasions, after the citation is concluded, the *Toldot Ya'akov Yosef* adds to this: ***kakh** shamati mimori,* "**This** is what I heard from my teacher." He was once asked to explain this apparent redundancy: Why does he begin with *shamati mimori* and at the end, on some occasions, does he add ***kakh** shamati mimori*? He very excitedly answered: if I am certain without a shadow of a doubt, if I feel fully attuned to what the rebbe said and how he said it, if I am sure that I completely appreciate the words, structure, and setting – then I will add *kakh shamati mimori.*

I would like to present another illustration of how the process of understanding a *ḥakham* is an ongoing one, both cognitively and experientially. The Gemara in Ḥagigah[13] tells us that R. Yoḥanan invited R. Elazar to study with him *sodei hatorah,* esoteric lore. He said to him, "Let me teach you *ma'aseh merkavah,* the insights, the principles, the truths of the metaphysical structure of our Torah." R. Elazar demurred: "I am not old enough." R. Elazar felt that he was not sufficiently advanced; he felt that he did not meet the stiff prerequisites that *Ḥazal* listed as mandatory for such study. When R. Elazar was older, R. Yoḥanan passed away, whereupon R. Assi extended a similar invitation to R. Elazar, using the very words of R. Yoḥanan: "Let me teach you *ma'aseh merkavah.*" R. Elazar's response was startling: "If my merit had been cumulatively great enough and was still operative, then I would have learned this from R. Yoḥanan."

... כל אלה זרים הם לשיטת ר' חיים היוצרת והנאמנה (הרב יוסף דב סולוביצ'יק, "מה דודך מדוד", **דברי הגות והערכה**, ההסתדרות הציונית העולמית תשמ"ב, עמ' 83).

13. אמר ליה רבי יוחנן לרבי אלעזר: תא אגמרך במעשה המרכבה! אמר ליה: לא קשאי. כי קש – נח נפשיה דרבי יוחנן. אמר ליה רבי אסי: תא ואגמרך במעשה מרכבה! – אמר ליה: אי זכאי – גמירתא מרבי יוחנן רבך (חגיגה יג, א).

I believe that R. Elazar's intention is as follows:[14] To study with a great rebbe is not temporally confined to the actual lesson, similar to Rashi's comment cited above.[15] R. Elazar here confessed, undoubtedly with some anguish, that had he been privileged to be a sensitive, attentive *talmid*, a *yosheiv lifnei ḥakhamim,* then even now, after the passing of R. Yoḥanan, he would still be benefiting from his instruction, which was marked by such versatility and virtuosity. "I would have been able to understand independently by virtue of what he taught me, for his teaching would continue to provide insights as well as details, intuition as well as information." R. Elazar here tells us that Torah study is like a seed that keeps growing, flourishing, and ripening. There is an ongoing, open-ended effect of *talmud Torah* which transcends the time of cognitive activity. "If I were meritorious, privileged, had I studied attentively, realizing how carefully textured and fully nuanced the *shiurim* of my rebbe were, I still would be learning from him now."

In short, a disciplined and sensitive learning experience is like a catalyst: it continues to energize and resonate long after the first burst of energy.

There is another remarkable passage in Ḥagigah that deals with the relationship between Rebbe, also known as Rabbeinu Hakadosh, and R. Ḥiyya, whom the Rambam tells us in his introduction to the *Mishneh Torah* was among the few students who received traditions from Rabbeinu Hakadosh and understood their implications.[16]

The Gemara says[17] that Rebbe and R. Ḥiyya went on a trip. When they reached their destination, an unnamed place, they inquired: "Is there a *talmid ḥakham* here in town? If so, let us go and greet him." They

---

14. עיינו ר׳ שלמה רבינוביץ מרדומסק, **תפארת שלמה**, ניו יורק תש״ע, מבוא השער עמ׳ לא

15. See above n. 8.

16. ואלו הם גדולי החכמים שהיו בבית דינו של רבינו הקדוש וקיבלו ממנו... ור׳ חייא ... ועמהם אלפים ורבבות משאר החכמים (**משנה תורה**, הקדמה).

17. רבי ורבי חייא הוו שקלי ואזלי באורחא, כי מטו לההוא מתא אמרי: איכא צורבא מרבנן הכא? נזיל וניקביל אפיה. אמרי: איכא צורבא מרבנן הכא, ומאור עינים הוא. אמר ליה רבי חייא לרבי: תיב את, לא תזלזל בנשיאותך, איזיל אנא ואקביל אפיה. תקפיה ואזל בהדיה. כי הוו מיפטרי מיניה אמר להו: אתם הקבלתם פנים הנראים ואינן רואין, תזכו להקביל פנים הרואים ואינן נראין. אמר ליה [רבי לרבי חייא]: איכו השתא מנעתן מהאי בירכתא. אמר ליה [רבי חייא]: ממאן שמיעא לך? – מפרקיה דרבי יעקב שמיע לי (חגיגה ה, ב ע״פ **עין יעקב**).

were told that there was a young scholar there who was blind. R. Ḥiyya, the devoted, solicitous *talmid*, said to Rebbe: "Stay here! Do not demean your high office. (*After all, Rabbeinu Hakadosh had concentrated in him the greatest spiritual and temporal powers. He had no equal. So R. Ḥiyya said that it is not appropriate.*) You stay here; I will go and greet the young scholar." Rebbe, however, was insistent and went with him. When they took leave of the blind *talmid ḥakham*, he turned to them and said: "You greeted one who is seen and does not see; may you be worthy to greet the One who sees and is not seen" (*a remarkable, extraordinary berakhah*).

Rebbe then turned to his devoted *talmid* and said: "Had I listened to you, had I let your solicitousness for my office, your sense of ceremonialism, prevail, you would have caused me to forfeit this *berakhah*." (*In other words, there is no substitute for this berakhah; you could not have been a messenger to bring it to me since it is formulated in direct address. Only those who actually came to greet the blind young scholar could receive that blessing.*) R. Ḥiyya then asked Rebbe: "How did you come to this *masorah*, this tradition?" (*That is, how is it that I, R. Ḥiyya, who follows you so closely, do not know this halakhah, this part of the masorah?*) The Gemara reports that Rebbe told him, mentioning someone whom we don't know from any other place, as the source for this halakhah.

Thus, R. Ḥiyya, for all his great knowledge of the *masorah* of Rebbe, realized that he did not understand his rebbe completely. He thought that Rebbe was concerned with ceremony, with pomp and circumstance, and therefore he said to him, "Don't demean your high office." He now realized that he was wrong. Secondly, he realized that there was always more to learn, which is why he asked him *miman shemi'a lakh*, "from whom did you hear this halakhah?" "What is the source of this halakhah?"

SHIMUSH ḤAKHAMIM – SERVING THE LEARNED

This is an enthralling story, and it suggests a new definition of the well-known concept of *shimush ḥakhamim*, usually translated "serving the learned." On the face of it, accompanying your teacher, your rebbe, on a trip should be classified as *shimush*. You help carry his valise, you see that he is dropped off right in front of the hotel or wherever he's going; that should be *shimush*. I am reminded of the stories told of the great *talmidim* of the Ba'al Shem Tov, who used to vie with each other to travel with him on certain trips, to go in his chariot with the famous *ba'al agalah*, wagon driver, of the Besht, Alexy. This is what R. Ḥiyya did when he went with R. Yehudah Hanasi; presumably this is *shimush*.

Let us revert for a moment to Reb Ḥayyim Volozhiner and recall what his son R. Itzeleh (in his introduction to the *Nefesh Haḥayyim*) recorded about his father's relation to the Gra:

> Even greater than his studies with him was the *shimush*, the service he provided.... [18]

The Gemara in Berakhot says something similar: "service (to a sage) is greater than study."[19] Reb Itzeleh however teaches something new by taking this Gemara one step further:

> Even greater than his studies with him was the *shimush* that he provided for his sainted rabbi. During those many days when he *amad lifanav*, stood before him – that is, on the face of it, engaging in *shimush* – the pathways of the exoteric Torah (*nigleh*) were illuminated, as well as the wondrous pathways of esoteric wisdom (*nistar*).[20]

Here *shimush* means learning, which is not as we would conventionally translate or define it. *Shimush* is another modality of *limmud*. *Shimush* is not only attending to the rebbe, as would appear from the Gemara that distinguishes between *lamad* and *yatzak mayim*, poured water (on his hands). *Shimush* is also assuring that the *talmid* has maximum exposure to the rebbe, that his understanding is constantly deepened and enhanced, that he is positioned to absorb everything. Thus, *amad lifanav*, this *shimush*, is what enabled the *talmid*, Reb Ḥayyim, to acquire his own

---

18. ויותר מלמודו היה גדול שמושו... (ר׳ יצחק מוולוז׳ין, הקדמה ל**נפש החיים**)

19. גדולה שמושה של תורה יותר מלמודה שנאמר: (מלכים ב׳ ג, יא) פֹּה אֱלִישָׁע בֶּן שָׁפָט אֲשֶׁר **יָצַק מַיִם** עַל יְדֵי אֵלִיָּהוּ, **למד לא נאמר אלא יצק** – מלמד שגדולה שמושה יותר מלמודה (ברכות ז, ב).

20. ויותר מלמודו היה גדול שמושו ששִׁמש את רבו החסיד נ״ע. ובימים הרבים שעמד לפניו אנהיר ליה שבילי דאורייתא בנגלה ונתיבות פליאות בנסתר (**נפש החיים**, למעלה הערה 18).

greatness in *nigleh* and *nistar*, "for the pathways of the exoteric Torah were illuminated, as well as the wondrous pathways of esoteric wisdom."

And hence R. Itzeleh continues:[21] "This is the significance of what Rebbe (R. Yehudah Hanasi) said: 'Had I seen R. Meir frontally,'" which means *re'iyat panim*, "seeing the face," so to speak. R. Itzeleh is referring to the Gemara in Eiruvin:

> R. Yehudah Hanasi said: The fact that I am more incisive than my colleagues is due to the fact that I saw R. Meir from behind. Had I seen him from the front, I would be even more incisive, as it is written: "And your eyes shall see your teacher."[22]

This allusion to "Had I seen him from the front," which is *re'iyat panim*, can be understood only metaphorically, as the Rambam understands it. It means comprehensive, precise understanding. It should not be taken literally to mean that R. Meir said: I saw R. Yehudah Hanasi only from a rear view, but had I had a frontal view – had I "seen his face" – then it would have made a difference for me. The metaphorical meaning of *re'iyat panim* is as the Rambam explains it in *Shemonah Perakim*:

> Moshe designates by the term "beholding the Divine face" the true comprehension of God, for when one sees another person face-to-face his features become imprinted upon his mind, so that he will not confuse him with others; whereas if he sees only his back, he may seemingly recognize him but will subsequently either be in doubt or even confuse him with others.[23]

---

21. הוא הוא דחזא רביה מקמיה וגליה ליה מסכתא ונהירו דחכמתא. (הקדמה **לנפש החיים**)

22. אמר רבי: האי דמחדדנא מחבראי - דחזיתיה לרבי מאיר מאחוריה; ואילו חזיתיה מקמיה – הוה מחדדנא טפי, דכתיב וְהָיוּ עֵינֶיךָ רֹאוֹת אֶת מוֹרֶיךָ (ישעיהו ל, כ; עירובין יג, ב).

    For further discussion, see pp. 32–35 and n. 52.

23. וכִנה את אמיתות ההשגה בראיית פנים, לפי שהאדם כאשר רואה פני חברו יקבע לו בלבו צורה שאינה מתחלפת בזולתו. אבל אם רואה אחוריו, אף על פי שהוא מכיר אותו באותה הראיה, אפשר ויסתפק בו ואפשר שיתחלף לו בזולתו. (רמב"ם, **שמונה פרקים**, פרק שביעי, **פירוש המשנה** בתרגום של הרב יוסף קאפח ,מוסד הרב קוק תשכ"ה, עמ' רס).

We have seen now two aspects of *shimush*. One is termed *shemi'ah,* learning an oral tradition, and that characterizes the *yosheiv lifnei ḥakhamim*. The second is *re'iyah,* learning by seeing, by observation. Both are components of *shimush,* which is none other than a mode of learning.

With regard to *re'iyah,* R. Ḥiyya on a trip with Rabbeinu Hakadosh, and Reb Ḥayyim Volozhiner attending to the Gra, both learned by observation, by seeing. Their *re'iyah* was the foundation of their understanding, of avoiding error and misinterpretation.

The Rambam in *Hilkhot De'ot* adds an important insight on *shimush* by *re'iyah.* He states:

> We are directed by a positive commandment to attach ourselves to the wise and their disciples in order to learn from their deeds: For we read, "You shall cleave to Him" (Devarim 10:20) – but can a human possibly cleave to the *Shekhinah*? The Sages explained this commandment as follows: "Attach yourself to the wise and their disciples."[24] So a person must try to marry a scholar's daughter, marry his daughter to a scholar, dine and drink with scholars, manage commerce for scholars, and join himself to them in all manner of association, as it is said: "To cleave to Him" (Devarim 11:22).[25]

The Rambam's formulation of this halakhah is ostensibly based on the following Gemara:

> Is it possible for a person to cleave to the *Shekhinah*? Rather, anyone who marries his daughter to a Torah scholar, and one who

24. Here you see, incidentally, a very important theme which I have omitted; how *talmidim* play a role in the crystallization of the new *ḥavurah,* of this new *masorah* community – *ḥakhamim vetalmideihem.*

25. מצות עשה לְהִדבק בחכמים ותלמידיהם כדי ללמוד ממעשיהם, כענין שנאמר וּבוֹ תִדְבָּק; וכי אפשר לאדם לְהִדבק בשכינה? אלא כך אמרו חכמים בפירוש מצוה זו: הִדבק בחכמים ותלמי־דיהם. לפיכך צריך אדם להשתדל שישא בת תלמיד חכם, וישיא בתו לתלמיד חכם, ולאכול ולשתות עם תלמידי חכמים, ולעשות פרקמטיא לתלמיד חכם ולהתחבר להן בכל מיני חבור שנאמר וּלְדָבְקָה בוֹ. וכן צוו חכמים ואמרו: והוי מתאבק בעפר רגליהם ושותה בצמא את דבריהם (**משנה תורה**, הלכות דעות ו, ב).

> manages commerce on behalf of Torah scholars, and one who seeks to benefit Torah scholars with his property – the verse ascribes to him credit as though he cleaves to the *Shekhinah*.[26]

The Rambam's formulation, however, is not a mere reproduction of the Gemara. The most significant difference is that the Rambam in this halakhah combines the *Sifrei* with this Gemara. The *Sifrei*, commenting on the verse in Devarim "to walk in all His ways and to cleave to Him," says:

> Can man possibly ascend in the heavens and cleave to fire?... [The verse must mean:] attach oneself to the wise and their students, and in this way I consider you to have risen to the heavens.[27]

Hence, attaching oneself to the wise and their students, and the need to serve and assist them are combined. The Rambam then concludes that halakhah with an important addition, a verbatim quotation from the Mishnah (Avot 1:4): "The Sages thus charged: 'Sit in the dust at their feet and drink thirstily their words.'"[28] Attaching oneself to them, serving them, associating with them and learning from them are all of a piece. The mitzvah of attaching oneself to the wise includes not only *shimush*, helping and assisting the wise,[29] but associating with them and learning from them as well.

According to the Rambam there is a double element of learning, which he presents explicitly in his *Sefer Hamitzvot*:

26. וכי אפשר לאדם לידבק בשכינה? אלא כל המשיא בתו לתלמיד חכם, והעושה פרקמטיא לתלמידי חכמים, והמהנה תלמידי חכמים מנכסיו – מעלה עליו הכתוב כאילו מדבק בשכינה (כתובות קיא, ב).
27. לָלֶכֶת בְּכָל דְּרָכָיו וּלְדָבְקָה בוֹ (דברים יא, כב) וכי היאך אפשר לאדם לעלות למרום ולדבק באש, [והלא כבר נאמר (דברים ד, כד) כִּי ה׳ אֱלֹקֶיךָ אֵשׁ אֹכְלָה הוּא]... אלא הדבק בחכמים ותלמידיהם, ומעלה אני עליך כאילו עלית למרום (**ספרי על ספר דברים**, עקב, פיסקא מט).
28. See the conclusion of the Rambam's halakhah in n. 25 above.
29. ראו למעלה הערה 26, ועיינו רש״י שם, ד״ה **העושה פרקמטיא**: מתעסק בממון ת״ח כדי להגיע לידם שכר והם פנויין לעסוק בתורה ע״י אלו.

> To model oneself according to their actions and to know the true opinions that are denoted by their words.[30]

This completely redefines the entire mitzvah of attaching oneself to the wise and their students. To use the language that the Rov taught us: the *ma'aseh hamitzvah,* the physical activity associated with the mitzvah, is what the Gemara in Ketubot refers to when it says: "who manages commerce on behalf of Torah scholars" and "who marries his daughter to a scholar." But the *kiyum hamitzvah,* the inner experiential fulfillment of the mitzvah of *shimush,* is to be in the company of Torah scholars – to see the wise as they are in order to "learn from their actions," *lilmod mima'aseihem,* as the Rambam significantly emphasizes. This phrase does not mean to imitate, but rather to adopt and adapt, everyone *kefi koḥo,* to the best of his ability, from what one sees and understands.

This entire concept is particularly significant in light of the following theme.

SUBJECTIVE PERCEPTIONS AND RELIGIOUS CONSCIOUSNESS

The scholar, the teacher – all his shyness and modesty, genuine humility and inner directedness, and avoidance of the public eye notwithstanding – reveals his inner spiritual life to his students.

He imparts spiritual insights, and touches his students with his faith and enthusiasm, with his religious experiences and yearnings. If we are sensitive, we see not only the workings of his mind, we glimpse not only the processes of his reasoning – the objective discursive exposition of the *Torah shebe'al peh* – but we are given the opportunity to see and share his subjective perceptions, his emotional existence, his religious consciousness and theological sensibility.

The Rambam in *Hilkhot Shabbat,* in summarizing the halakhah of honoring the Shabbat, states:

30. כדי שנגיע לנו בכך להדמות במעשיהם ולדעת הסברות האמתיות מדבריהם (**ספר המצוות לרמב"ם**, מוסד הרב קוק תשל"א, מצות עשה ו).

> What is meant by "honor"? The Sages explained that each person should wash his face, hands, and feet with hot water... and be seated with solemnity in expectation of the Shabbat.... The ancient Sages used to assemble their disciples on Friday, put on their best clothes, and say: "Come, let us go out to meet Shabbat the King."[31]

For what purpose did the earlier scholars assemble their students? It could not have been for a *shiur*, for we know that the halakhah is that children do not study Torah on the eve before Shabbat and holidays.[32] They were assembled not for study, but for the purpose of religious experience. The *ḥakhamim* would declare, "Come, let us go out to meet Shabbat the King."

The *ma'aseh hamitzvah*, the concrete act of honoring the Shabbat, is accomplished by each person washing his hands and feet in hot water, enwrapped in a tallit and seated with solemnity to anticipate the coming of the Shabbat. The *kiyum hamitzvah*, the inner fulfillment, is receiving Shabbat the King. The teacher takes the lead in preparing his students to encounter and experience Shabbat.

The Rambam provides another example at the end of *Hilkhot Shofar Vesukkah Velulav* of how the scholar imparts spiritual insights and touches his students with his enthusiasm and his religious experiences:

> It is a religious duty to intensify one's joy on this occasion. Ignorant individuals, or just anybody who wished [to participate] took no leading part in it. Only great Jewish scholars, heads of academies, members of the Sanhedrin, elders, and men of piety and good deeds danced, clapped hands, played music, and

---

31. איזהו כבוד? זה שאמרו חכמים שמצוה על האדם לרחוץ פניו ידיו ורגליו בחמין... ויושב בכובד ראש ומיחל להקבלת פני השבת... חכמים הראשונים היו מקבצין תלמידיהן בערב שבת ומתעטפים ואומרים בואו ונצא לקראת שבת המלך (**משנה תורה**, הלכות שבת ל, ב).

32. ולא יבטלו התינוקות כלל חוץ מערבי שבתות וימים טובים (**משנה תורה** הלכות תלמוד תורה ב, ב).

> entertained in the Temple in the days of Sukkot. Everyone else… came to watch and listen.[33]

What were they coming to see? It was not a spectacle. They came to fulfill the two components of the *masorah*, to see and hear. They came to gain deeper spiritual understanding by observing how the *ḥakhamim* revealed their emotions to the people, how they showed the people through their actions what it means to rejoice before the Lord, what the halakhah of *simḥah yeteirah*, of intense joy on Sukkot, means.[34] This is part of a natural, integrated, and calibrated transmission of Torah, transmission of knowledge together with insight and experience.

The *ḥakham* reveals much that is otherwise hidden: his ethical behavior; his spiritual yearning; the emotional, experiential components of his religious commitment. All of this – and at times this is difficult for the rebbe – is done in order that the *talmid* will be the beneficiary. The intellectual sophistication is harmoniously integrated with the religious sensitivity and the experiential intensity.

I believe that for all the Rov's emphasis on the notion of the hidden and unknown nature of God, for all his moving depictions of the hidden character of *gedolei Yisrael* such as his *hespedim* of the Brisker Rov and R. Ḥayyim Heller and in his descriptions of the *Ish Hahalakhah* – and of course the autobiographic resonance in the latter is unmistakable – the Rov did reveal himself. I wish to emphasize, however, that when all is said and done, more is concealed than revealed. It has to be this way, as *Ḥazal* said: "However, [regarding] Torah scholars themselves, no one has laid eyes [upon them], aside from You, O God."[35] No matter how much they reveal themselves, they are still a great mystery. We need only to remember him as he was, as he lives in our eternal *masorah*, to study his Torah; and this honest disciplined remembrance will enable us to forgo

33. מצוה להרבות בשמחה זו. ולא היו עושין אותה עמי הארץ וכל מי שרוצה, אלא גדולי חכמי ישראל וראשי הישיבות והחסידים והזקנים ואנשי מעשה, הם שהיו מרקדין ומספקין ומנגנין ומשמחין במקדש בימי חג הסוכות. אבל כל העם... באין לראות ולשמוע (**משנה תורה** הלכות שופר, סוכה ולולב ח, יד).

34. אף על פי שכל המועדות מצוה לשמוח בהן, בחג הסוכות היתה שם במקדש שמחה יתירה (**משנה תורה** הלכות שופר וסוכה ולולב ח, יב).

35. אבל תלמידי חכמים עצמם, עַיִן לֹא רָאָתָה אֱלֹקִים זוּלָתְךָ. (ישעיהו סד, ג; ברכות לד, ב)

fruitless speculation and to dispense with hypothesizing. Remember how well Reb Ḥayyim Volozhiner knew the inner spiritual life of the Gra. In fact, without Reb Ḥayyim Volozhiner, we would not begin to know anything about this aspect of the Gra. R. Avraham Yitzchak Hakohen Kook actually wrote that it was Reb Ḥayyim Volozhiner who revealed to us the Gra.[36] For Reb Ḥayyim this was part of his *limmud,* of his *shimush*; he knew, he observed, and therefore he could reveal.

THE ROV: THE CENTRALITY OF RELIGIOUS CONSCIOUSNESS

There are many aspects of the Rov that need to be understood. I will comment on his style of writing and on two very important themes: The Rov's relation to general culture and to the centrality of religious consciousness.

[The last two topics are covered in an almost identical manner in R. Twersky's *hesped* of the Rov that appears in chapter 5 (pp. 140–151). We have removed them from this *shiur* to avoid repetition but have retained here his important additional observations on religious consciousness. Please see his formulation there.]

The style of his writing is important. *Ḥazal* say, "Many prophets have visions about the same subject, but no two prophets will prophesy using the same style of expression,"[37] and this applies to the style of the Rov. His is a blend of biographical reflections, autobiographical allusions, anecdotal references, together with massive philosophic learning and perspicacity. My wife observed that the stories that he told about his father, grandfathers, and his mother all had a spiritual-halakhic purposiveness; I define it as the "teleology of storytelling." He didn't just talk about the *beit harav*, and he wasn't bragging about his *yiḥus*. This same purposiveness determined which philosophic concepts he used and in what context he used them. Just as there is a teleology of storytelling, there is also a teleology of analytic writing. His extraordinary style reflects an extraordinary mind and person.

---

36. **שיחות הראי"ה ואורות משנתו**, בעריכת משה צבי נריה, מורשת תשל"ט, עמ' רו

37. סגנון אחד עולה לכמה נביאים, ואין שני נביאים מתנבאים בסגנון אחד. (סנהדרין פט, א)

What fascinated him most was the religious consciousness. All his themes, which were presented with the utmost sophistication, with unmatched philosophic erudition, eloquence of style, and exposition, are essentially religious. His point of departure was not formal philosophy of religion, which he had mastered, but a glorious *masorah* of knowledge of God and love of God, a *masorah* in which the dialectic of ideas provides a natural setting for the primary immediate religious experience. The impetus and objective of all his writing is religious – "as a deer yearns for streams of water."[38]

There is so much that can be understood only if it is related to this theme, this perspective, of the centrality of the religious experience in its broadest sense. His criticism of Modern Orthodoxy should be seen from this perspective. He writes about when he would go to visit R. Ḥayyim Heller:

> When I visited him at home, on the West Side of Manhattan, with its congeries of bustling hollow Jewish life; with its synagogues, societies, clubs and their auxiliaries, I always felt as if I were entering another world, as if I had breached some border separating two realms of being – the domain of earlier generations of the *Shakh*, the *Taz* and the *Gra*, and that of modern Orthodoxy, with its snipped wings, unable to soar, unable to rise above the mundane, and its rootlessness, unable to fathom the depths of religious experience.[39]

---

38. כְּאַיָּל תַּעֲרֹג עַל אֲפִיקֵי מָיִם. (תהלים מב, ב)

39. "A Eulogy for R. Ḥayyim Heller," translated from the Hebrew by Shalom Carmy, in *Shiurei Harav: A Conspectus of the Public Lectures of Rabbi Joseph B. Soloveitchik*, ed. Joseph Epstein (Ktav, 1994), 54.
כשהייתי מבקרו במעונו, במערבה של מנהטן, על כל חשרת החיים היהודיים הסואנים והנבוכים שבה; על כל בתי־כניסיותיה, חברותיה, מועדוניה ואביזריהם, הייתי מרגיש תמיד, כאילו נכנסתי לעולם אחר, כאילו הבקעתי את הגבול המבדיל בין שתי רשויות קיום – רשות דורות ראשונים – הש"ך, הט"ז והגר"א – ורשותה של האורתודוקסיה המודרנית קצוצת הכנפיים להגביה עוף ונטולת השורשים לחדור לעומק החוויה הדתית. (הרב יוסף דב סולוביצ'יק, "פליטת סופריהם", **דברי הגות והערכה** ההסתדרות הציונית העולמית תשמ"ב, עמ' 148).
See also below, pp. 111–112.

I conclude with a story that is very significant. I remember clearly one Friday morning in 1963, I came to my father-in-law for our weekly learning, and the Rov came out to greet me, visibly excited and holding something, and he said to me: "I had such a surprise last night." He was holding a little book, *Kitvei Ha'ilui Meirakov*.[40] The Rakover Ilui – R. Avraham Eliyahu ben Moshe Mordechai Kaplan – he told me, was part of his folklore. Reb Ḥayyim Brisker used to say that had he lived a normal life span (he died at the age of thirty-two), he would have surpassed R. Akiva Eiger. The slim little volume that contained whatever was left of the *ḥiddushim* of the *ilui* was very similar to the *Bei'ur Hagra* – it includes brief notes that were not elaborated upon. What excited the Rov was that at the end of the book there are religious poems. The author, the Rakover Ilui, introduces these poems, *shirei kodesh,* by saying: "I am moved by my zeal for the holy tongue." He goes on to talk about the revival of the Hebrew language:

> In my zeal I have taken pen and ink … and I say … let us redouble our efforts for the language of our people and the tongue of our God … and see … that the grave of the ancient dead language has been opened … the breath of life has been blown into it and it has become a living language, a spoken tongue. … Songs of the soul are being sung and profound thoughts are being expressed in that language, loftier than poetry of other languages.

And he goes on to say:

> Those who in their astonishment have constantly proclaimed, "How is it possible to revive the dead," will now wrap themselves in shame. They see that until now this ancient language has subsisted in deep darkness like a corpse, with no one accountable. Upon reflecting on this, the spirit of song has surged from within me.[41]

---

40. ר׳ אברהם אליהו בן משה מרדכי קפלן, **כתבי העלוי מראקוב** (מביא לדפוס צבי קפלן, חלק ב, תשכ״ג, עמ׳ קעג ואילך).

41. קנא קנאתי לשפה הקדושה... ובקנאתי לקחתי עט ודיו... ואומר... חזקו ונתחזק בעד שפת עמנו ולשון אלקינו... ועתה לכו חזו... כי נפתח קבר השפה הנושנה הזאת המתה ... וינפח בה רוח

The Rakover Ilui intended these religious poems of his to be an expression of and a contribution to this revived affection for and appreciation of the holy tongue. The Rov told me that this casts a new light upon him and upon Volozhin. The Rakover Ilui wrote this during his years in Volozhin; he didn't live long enough to go much beyond that.

The Rov's excitement was visible, palpable; you could feel it, you could touch it. What was significant was this added expression of religious feeling, of religious consciousness.

"As a deer yearns for streams of water, so I yearn for You, O God."[42] This verse truly reflects the Rov's passionate longing for God.

What I have presented here is but a small fraction of the manifest portrait of his image, his identity.[43]

חיים ותהי לשפה חיה, לשון מדברת ... גם ישירו בה שירי־נפש והגיונים גבוהים, נעלים גם משירי שפות אחרות ... ועתה יעטו כמעיל בשתם המתפלאים תמיד ושואלים ״תחית המתים מן התורה מאין?״ הן עתה עיניהם תחזינה כי היתה השפה הקדומה הזאת, אשר במחשכים שכנה עד הנה כמתי־עולם ונחנו מהז כדַברי זאת החל רוח־השיר לפעמני... (קפלן, שם עמ׳ קעד).

42. See n. 38 above.

43. ״זה מקצת מדמות דיוקנו של הרב שנראה אצלנו״ [על פי דברי הסיום של הרב **באיש ההלכה**: ״אלא הם מקצת דרכיו של איש ההלכה. יותר ממה שהעליתי על הגליון כאן כתוב בתודעתו״, הרב יוסף דוב סולוביצ׳יק, **איש ההלכה גלוי ונסתר**, ההסתדרות הציונית העולמית, תשל״ט, עמ׳ 113.]

עשו סְיָג לתורה

Chapter 4

Make a Fence Around the Torah

SEYAG, A FENCE THAT ENHANCES AND DEEPENS

The third saying of the *Anshei Knesset Hagedolah* in the opening mishnah of *Pirkei Avot* is *asu seyag latorah*, "make a fence around the Torah."[1] My objective here is to demonstrate that the conventional understanding of this saying is not adequate, but needs to be emended or expanded. In the course of the analysis I will integrate many diverse sources and themes in Halakhah and Aggadah.

1. [Rabbi Twersky opened this *shiur* with the following direct address to the audience: A previous *shiur* in memory of *maran harav* (ch. 1) was devoted to an analysis of the phrase *ha'amidu talmidim harbeh*, "raise up many disciples," the second saying of the *Anshei Knesset Hagedolah* that appears in *Pirkei Avot*. It was not a eulogy nor did it contain any rhetorical, personal, *ad hominem* amplifications concerning the Rov. Nevertheless, it was a personal tribute, because the Rov's learning underlies just about every aspect of our ongoing *talmud Torah*, and his deep-seated piety, benevolence, and humility illustrate and concretize the noblest principles of our *masorah*. Our ability to penetrate to the inner strata of Torah and to achieve new insights is an outgrowth of his Torah teaching, his instruction, and his stimulation, which, needless to say, continue posthumously.]

Actually, the three epigrams of the *Anshei Knesset Hagedolah* have one common denominator, one goal: a determination to arrive at the truth.

1. "Be deliberate in judgment": This is a warning against being impulsive or impetuous in the process of study and in reaching conclusions from that study.

2. "Raise up many disciples": Many disciples bring multiple talents and large reservoirs of knowledge to bear on the study of Torah. There is no monopoly on Torah study, and there should not be any monopoly. The more people involved in the study of Torah, the greater the chance of arriving at the truth.

3. "Make a fence around the Torah": This part also shares a common denominator with the other two parts – namely, the pursuit of truth.

Seyag is usually translated as a fence, a hedge, some external force or entity that is protective of something else. This translation is based on the way *Ḥazal* interpret the verse in Vayikra, *ushmartem et mishmarti*, "you shall keep My charge, not to engage in any of the abhorrent practices that were done before you, and you shall not defile yourselves through them; I am the Lord your God."[2] Because of the common practice in Hebrew of using a verb and a noun from the same root, *Ḥazal* were led to interpret *ushmartem* not as "guard or preserve that which I have commanded," but rather, *asu mishmeret lemishmarti*,[3] "establish a safeguard for My charge," that is, take an active step. That changes the meaning of the two words. It is interesting that almost none of the major commentators to the Torah interpret this verse according to *Ḥazal*, but rather according to what seems to them the simple meaning of the verse.

In truth, *seyag* can be understood in two ways. The first is as a fence or a hedge that is protective in a restrictive sense. An example of this is the first mishnah in *Berakhot*, where the time for the reading of *Shema* is set in order *leharḥik adam min ha'aveirah*, "to distance a person from transgression."[4] *Leharḥik* is the key word according to the restrictive

2. וּשְׁמַרְתֶּם אֶת מִשְׁמַרְתִּי לְבִלְתִּי עֲשׂוֹת מֵחֻקּוֹת הַתּוֹעֵבֹת אֲשֶׁר נַעֲשׂוּ לִפְנֵיכֶם וְלֹא תִטַּמְּאוּ בָּהֶם אֲנִי ה׳ אֱלֹקֵיכֶם (ויקרא יח, ל).

3. עשו משמרת למשמרתי. (מועד קטן ה, א)

4. להרחיק אדם מן העבירה. (משנה ברכות א, א)

understanding of *asu seyag*, "make a fence." Similarly, in tractate Ḥullin we find "distance yourself (*harḥek*) from unseemliness and from things similar to it."[5] Anytime we have *leharḥik*, distance or space is created to ensure proper observance; the objective is that you not trespass. This is the restrictive understanding of "make a fence around the Torah."

Seyag, however, not only protects but also enhances and deepens, it elaborates and amplifies. *Seyag*, in other words, has not only a constrictive meaning but a positive, expansive meaning as well.

Actually, the formulation of "to distance a person from transgression" already seems to suggest this. In fact, the Gemara cited above, *asu mishmeret lemishmarti*, "you must establish a safeguard for My charge," continues with an additional verse:

> Ravina said: 'And to him who orders his way (*vesam derekh*) I will show the salvation of God" (Tehillim 50:3); R. Yehoshua ben Levi said: Whoever appraises (*sham*) his ways merits seeing the salvation of the Holy One, blessed be He, as it is stated: "And to him who orders his way." Do not read it as *vesam*, "who orders"; rather, read it as *vesham*, "appraises"; to him will I show the salvation of God.[6]

The Gemara here uses the well-known method of *al tikrei*, which introduces a slight orthographic change in the biblical text in order to provide a new insight into the verse. By changing the reading of ***vesam** derekh* to ***vesham** derekh*, the verse now reads that one must appraise one's ways. This is a support for the halakhah *asu mishmeret lemishmarti*, "establish a safeguard for My charge," in which a very different conception emerges. *Asu mishmeret* is now interpreted to mean "you appraise your ways," *vesham*, you evaluate the consequences of every action, and you try to have a proper perspective which will help you determine what to do and, just as important, how to do it.

---

5. הרחק מן הכיעור ומן הדומה לו. (חולין מד, ב)

6. רבינא אמר: וְשָׂם דֶּרֶךְ אַרְאֶנּוּ בְּיֵשַׁע אֱלֹקִים (תהלים נ, כג). אמר ר יהושע בן לוי: כל הַשָּׁם אורחותיו זוכה ורואה בישועתו של הקב"ה שנאמר וְשָׂם דרך אל תקרי וְשָׂם אלא וְשָׁם דרך אראנו בישע אלקים (מועד קטן ה, א).

Actually, we can be very precise and anchor the two interpretations concerning the proper characterization of *seyag* in two formulations of the Rambam: one in his *Commentary on the Mishnah* and the other in *Hilkhot Mamrim.*

In the Rambam's commentary to the first Mishnah in Avot, in explaining *asu seyag latorah,* he quotes the Gemara in Mo'ed Katan:

> "Make a fence around the Torah" – the fence consists of *gezerot,* edicts, and *takkanot,* ordinances, which will distance a person from transgression, as it is written: "You shall keep My charge"; Ḥazal have said: You must establish a safeguard for My charge.[7]

In *Hilkhot Mamrim,* however, while describing the interpretive and legislative prerogatives of the Sanhedrin, the Rambam lists the various categories of the Oral Law, including "regulations that were enacted to protect the Torah according to the needs of the time, which includes *gezerot,* edicts, *takkanot,* ordinances, and *minhagot,* customs."[8] The key change is the addition of the term *minhagot.* In his *Commentary on the Mishnah,* the Rambam mentions only *gezerot* and *takkanot,* while here he adds *minhagot.* As I will explain shortly, our entire understanding of *seyag* is changed by the inclusion of this category.

In order to avoid generalization, we will clarify the importance of this distinction through two examples: one, the laws of Shabbat, a topic of intrinsic importance, very significant in its own right; the other is the trait of silence.

SHABBAT

Shabbat exists on two levels. There is the rigorous observance of Shabbat, and there is the fully nuanced appreciation of the meaning and impact of Shabbat. The *Zohar* calls it *raza deshabbat,* the secret, the inner

---

7. "ועשו סיָג לתורה" – רוצה לומר **הגזרות והתקנות** אשר ירחיקו את האדם מן העבירה, כמו שאמר יתעלה וּשְׁמַרְתֶּם אֶת מִשְׁמַרְתִּי ואמרו בפירוש זה "עשו משמרת למשמרתי" (רמב"ם **פירוש המשנה**, אבות א, א).

8. דברים שעשאום סיָג לתורה ולפי מה שהשעה צריכה, והן **הגזרות והתקנות והמנהגות** (**משנה תורה** הלכות ממרים א, ב).

meaning of Shabbat, the Shabbat that can be *experienced,* not *observed* by refraining from the thirty-nine *melakhot,* types of work. These are the two levels of Shabbat.

The Rambam in *Hilkhot Shabbat,* chapter 21 tells us of an entire category of actions that are prohibited because of *shvut* even though they are not part of the thirty-nine *melakhot*:

> It is written in the Torah, "you shall rest," implying that one must refrain even from doing things that are not actual work. There are many things which the Sages prohibited on the basis of *shvut.* Some are forbidden because they resemble prohibited kinds of work; others are forbidden as a preventive measure for fear that they may result in doing work that is forbidden under the penalty of stoning.[9]

Thus, *shvut* is classified as an activity that resembles *melakhah* but is not one of the thirty-nine *melakhot* defined as *mide'oraita,* scripturally proscribed, and as the Rambam emphasized, "There are many things which the Sages prohibited on the basis of *shvut.*"

In chapter 24 of *Hilkhot Shabbat,* the Rambam introduces a further dimension concerning the proper appreciation of Shabbat:

> Some acts are forbidden on Shabbat even though they neither resemble nor lead to prohibited work.[10]

What is this new category? The usual understanding of this last citation is that it is a continuation of the previous discussion in chapter 21 and presents another category of *shvut,* but that is not so. The Rambam is quite emphatic and unequivocal that "they neither resemble nor lead

9. נאמר בתורה תִּשְׁבֹּת – אפילו מדברים שאינן מלאכה חייב לשבות מהן. ודברים הרבה הן שאסרו חכמים משום שבות: מהן דברים אסורים מפני שהן דומים למלאכות ומהן דברים אסורים גזרה שמא יבוא מהן איסור סקילה (**משנה תורה** הלכות שבת כא, א).

10. יש דברים שהן אסורים בשבת, אף על פי שאינם דומין למלאכה ואינם מביאין לידי מלאכה (שם, כד, א).

to prohibited work." The Avnei Nezer[11] says that the Rambam in chapter 24 is not relating to *shvut,* and his words cannot be subsumed under that category. In fact, from the point of view of the severity of violation of *melakhot,* those activities of chapter 24 are less stringent than those mentioned as categories of *shvut* in the preceding three chapters. However, they are more meaningful regarding the proper appreciation of Shabbat. The prohibitions of chapter 21 fall under the first category of *seyag,* the restrictive category, that is, *gezerot* and *takkanot,*[12] "things forbidden because they resemble prohibited kinds of work." Those in chapter 24 are different. As the Rambam himself states there:

> Why then were they forbidden? Because it is written: "If you refrain from following your business on Shabbat, on My holy day," and it is written: "If you honor it, not following your wonted ways, not pursuing your business, nor speaking of it" (Yeshayahu 58:13).[13]

Take note that he quotes the verse in two parts. The key is the second half of the verse, which is the main determinant for understanding chapter 24. You honor Shabbat by being careful and by not doing things you would ordinarily do, "not following your wonted ways, not pursuing your business, nor *speaking of it.*" What is very new here is that one can violate Shabbat even by improper speech. Even idle talk infringes upon the sanctity of Shabbat.

These additional prohibitions that the Rambam lists in chapter 24 convert Shabbat from a day of rest into a day of holiness. The *melakhot* and the category of *shvut* relate to the character of Shabbat as a day of rest, but minimally to Shabbat as a day of holiness. The sanctity of Shabbat which we proclaim at the beginning of Shabbat in *Kiddush* – "Remember

---

11. It is noted in passing by the Avnei Nezer in a parenthetical remark:
מפרק כ״א עד פרק כ״ד מונה והולך סדר השבותים. יש שהם דומין למלאכה, ויש שמא יבוא לידי מלאכה. ואחר כך בפרק כ״ד יש דברים שאסרו חכמים אף שאין דומין למלאכה ואין מביאין לידי מְלאכה. ומפני מה נאסרו משום שנאמר מִמְּצוֹא חֶפְצְךָ וְדַבֵּר דָּבָר. הרי דאינו שבות (שו״ת אבני נזר חלק אורח חיים סימן מג).

12. See nn. 7, 8 above.

13. ומפני מה נאסרו? משום שנאמר: אִם תָּשִׁיב מִשַּׁבָּת רַגְלֶךָ עֲשׂוֹת חֲפָצֶיךָ בְּיוֹם קָדְשִׁי, ונאמר: וְכִבַּדְתּוֹ מֵעֲשׂוֹת דְּרָכֶיךָ מִמְּצוֹא חֶפְצְךָ וְדַבֵּר דָּבָר (**משנה תורה** הלכות שבת כד, א).

it through praise and sanctification,"[14] as the Rambam says in chapter 29 – is not reflected directly or indirectly in the long list of *melakhot.* But the additional prohibitions that emerge from the verse that the Rambam cites in chapter 24, "If you honor it, not following your wonted ways, not pursuing your business, nor speaking of it," create a day of holiness. They are not merely a fence for protection; they are rather defined by the Rambam as follows: "Some acts are forbidden on Shabbat even though they *neither resemble nor lead to prohibited work.*"[15] They have nothing to do with the thirty-nine *melakhot,* and cannot be characterized as a fence or a hedge. They are a *seyag* in the sense of enhancing or expanding the significance and meaning of Shabbat. They finish shaping or sculpting the Shabbat.

It is because of this dimension of *seyag,* which enhances and expands the meaning of Shabbat, that all the prohibitions of Shabbat are put into an appropriate framework. The inner experience that one is supposed to have on Shabbat, and of Shabbat, is sketched against the background of specific *melakhot.*

I want to add here a new insight by way of elaboration. The Rambam's definition for the laws of honoring Shabbat is found only at the very end of *Hilkhot Shabbat.* In chapter 30, the Rambam speaks about "honor and delight":

> Four things have been enjoined regarding Shabbat: two on biblical authority, and two on the authority of the Sages and clearly expressed by the Prophets. The Torah says: *Remember* (Shemot 20:8) and *observe* (Devarim 5:12); the Prophets elaborated on *honor* and *delight,* as it is written: "Call Shabbat a delight, and the LORD's sacred day an honor" (Yeshayahu 58:13).[16]

14. זכרהו זכירת שבח וקידוש. (שם פרק כט, א)

15. שאינם דומין למלאכה ואינם מביאין לידי מלאכה. (למעלה הערה 10)

16. ארבעה דברים נאמרו בשבת: שניים מן התורה; ושניים מדברי סופרים, והן מפורשין על ידי הנביאים. שבתורה: זָכוֹר ושָׁמוֹר; ושנתפרשו על ידי הנביאים: כִּבוּד ועונג, שנאמר וְקָרָאתָ לַשַּׁבָּת עֹנֶג, לִקְדוֹשׁ ה' מְכֻבָּד (**משנה תורה** הלכות שבת ל, א). השוו הרב יוסף דב סולובייצ'יק, "כיבוד ועונג שבת", **שיעורים לזכר אבא מרי ז"ל**, מוסד הרב קוק תשס"ג, עמ' סד-פג.

"Remember" refers to the recital of *Kiddush*, and "observe" refers to the entire realm of the laws of Shabbat that prohibit work. The two that the prophets elaborated on and clarified were *kibbud* and *oneg*, "honor" and "delight." What exactly is "honoring the Shabbat"? How is it fulfilled? The common aspect of the examples the Rambam gives is based upon a sense of expectation, of emotional anticipation for the coming of Shabbat or specific preparations that we do before Shabbat. This is what differentiates *kibbud*, "honor," from *oneg*, "delight." Delight takes place on Shabbat, and honor is expressed in preparation for Shabbat.

In light of chapter 24, I want to suggest that there is a second kind of "honoring the Shabbat" which the Rambam cites: "If you honor it, not following your wonted ways, not pursuing your business, nor speaking of it."[17] This honor is like delight; it manifests itself *on* Shabbat, through a special sensitivity of behavior and a refinement of speech. In other words, while all other aspects of Shabbat are rigorously and meticulously defined, this honoring is open-ended. It is not only a preparation *before* Shabbat, but it is reflected in one's behavior, particularly in one's speech *during* Shabbat. Honoring is thus a symbol of this heightened sensitivity that expresses itself in one's behavior and speech on Shabbat.

In chapter 30, halakhah 6, the Rambam says that everyone without exception has the obligation to prepare for Shabbat:

> Even a person of high rank, who does not as a rule buy things at the market or engage in household chores, should himself perform what is necessary for Shabbat, for this is his way of showing respect.[18]

After giving examples of great scholars who would chop wood for Shabbat as well as cook the meals and do the shopping, the Rambam concludes, "The more one honors Shabbat in this manner, the more praise

---

17. See n. 13 above.

18. אף על פי שיהיה אדם חשוב ביותר, ואין דרכו ליקח דברים מן השוק ולא להתעסק במלאכות שבבית – חייב לעשות דברים שהן לצורך השבת בגופו, שזה הוא כבודו (**משנה תורה** הלכות שבת ל, ו). השוו: ואין הגדולה והכבוד אלא לשמוח לפני ה' (שם הלכות שופר וסוכה ולולב ח, טו).

he deserves."[19] In halakhah 7 he adds: "The more one spends for Shabbat and for the preparation of a variety of tasty foods, the more praise he deserves."[20]

You can understand well that you will not find anywhere a phrase like "the more one keeps the laws of Shabbat the more praise he deserves." That is impossible and nonsensical, since observing the laws of Shabbat refers to clearly defined and delimited activities. *Meḥitzot,* halakhic partitions, provide an example; one cannot change the nature of the partitions which define private property. If the partition conforms to the halakhic requirement, then there is a private area by definition. You cannot change the definition of what constitutes cooking on Shabbat. If you do a certain kind of activity which cooks raw food up to a certain point, which makes it edible – be it a third or half cooked, whatever the definition is – then you have violated the prohibition against cooking. If you refrain from cooking, you cannot say, "Whoever increases his *not-cooking* on Shabbat is praiseworthy!" That statement is impossible to formulate; it is jarring to hear, because it makes no sense.

The same goes for remembering the Shabbat by reciting *Kiddush.* One cannot say, "Whoever increases his recital of *Kiddush* is praiseworthy," because the Halakhah clearly defines in precise terms what it means to "sanctify Shabbat with words," and we cannot add to that. It would therefore make no sense to say, "Whoever increases the mentioning of Shabbat is praiseworthy."[21] You cannot have such a statement, because it refers to finite, carefully delimited activities. Honor and delight, however, are open-ended categories. They refer to one's experience of Shabbat, and here I am including the honor of chapter 24 as well – "If you honor it, not following your wonted ways, not pursuing your business,

19. וכל המרבה בדבר זה – הרי זה משובח (הלכות שבת ל, ו). השוו: וכל המרבה לספר ביציאת מצרים הרי זה משובח (הגדה של פסח).

20. וכל המרבה בהוצאת שבת ובתיקון מאכלים רבים וטובים – הרי זה משובח (שם הלכות שבת ל, ז).

21. פוסק הרמב"ם (**משנה תורה** הלכות שבת ב, יז) נפלה דליקה, ויש שם אדם שחוששין שמא ישרף – מכבין אותה להצילו מן האש, ואף על פי שהוא כובש דרך ומתקנה בשעת כיבוי. **וכל הקודם להציל – הרי זה משובח, ואינו צריך ליטול רשות מבית דין בכל דבר שיש בו סכנה.** יש כאן דוגמה נוספת של עשייה "משובחת" התלויה ביוזמה אישית ולא לפי קביעה הלכתית־משפטית.

nor speaking of it." This is open-ended, and therefore the Rambam does say – and it makes sense to say, as just mentioned – "The more one spends for Shabbat and for the preparation of a variety of tasty foods, the more praise he deserves."[22]

In light of all this, the Rambam's emphatic formulation at the conclusion of *Hilkhot Shabbat* makes good sense: "Anyone who observes Shabbat *according to its law*, and honors it and delights in it *according to his ability*."[23] The Rambam here is fastidious in his formulation. The observance of Shabbat is implemented according to its law, according to the objective norms of Halakhah, for that is all that we can do, and all that is expected of us to do. The difference comes in honor and delight.

That is why the Rambam says, "Whoever honors it and delights in it *according to his ability*." In *Hilkhot Tefillah*, the Rambam uses the similar phrase *lefi koḥo*, according to his ability, because there is room for a wide spectrum of experiences in prayer.[24] The Rambam also uses the phrase *kefi hasagat yado*, "(one gives charity) according to his means,"[25] which is similar to *kefi koḥo*, because only the minimum is defined, but beyond that it is open-ended. The same, of course, is the case with *talmud Torah*, the profundity of which is such that one will understand it according to his ability.[26]

What is remarkable but not surprising is the usage of the phrase here. One observes Shabbat according to its laws; but one honors it according to his ability, because honoring is open-ended. That is the *raza deshabbat*, the experience of the inner Shabbat, the secret – that which is not openly revealed – that which everybody will perceive in accord with his or her approach, with his or her perception and thinking about Shabbat.

What are we to say of a person who does not have this perspective of Shabbat, who does not understand the halakhot in chapter 21 in

---

22. See n. 20 above.

23. כל המשמר את השבת **כהלכתה**, ומכבדה ומענגה **כפי כחו**. (**משנה תורה** הלכות שבת ל, טו)

24. שיהא אדם מתחנן ומתפלל בכל יום ומגיד שבחו של הקדוש ברוך הוא, ואחר כך שואל צרכיו שהוא צריך להם בבקשה ובתחנה, ואחר כך נותן שבח והודיה לה׳ על הטובה שהשפיע לו כל אחד **לפי כחו** (**משנה תורה** הלכות תפילה ונשיאת כפים א, ב).

25. נותן לו כפי השגת ידו. (**משנה תורה** הלכות מתנות עניים ז, ה)

26. See pp. 15–16. See *Torah of the Mind* (above, p. 3, n. 3), 133–138.

the Rambam, the halakhot of *shvut*, and particularly those in chapter 24 that the Rambam introduced as halakhot that are not *shvut* but are of great importance for the significance and understanding of the Shabbat? Consider, for example, halakhah 12 in chapter 24:

> The Sages forbade moving some things on Shabbat in the way that one does on weekdays. What was their reason for enacting this prohibition? They said, "And just like the prophets admonished and commanded that your walking on Shabbat not be like your walking on weekdays and that the speech of Shabbat not be like the speech of weekdays – as it is stated (Yeshayahu 58:13), "nor speaking of it" – all the more so should carrying on Shabbat not be like carrying on weekdays, so that it not be like a weekday in his eyes.[27]

If one were to lack this perspective of Shabbat, one could keep busy all day long without technically violating the Shabbat.

What is such a person? What is the status of a person who does not understand how Shabbat should impact on his personality? The Ramban in Vayikra calls him a *naval bireshut hatorah*.[28] He does not say that one who, for example, moves furniture around all day long is a sinner, liable for excision or a sin-offering, but rather he calls him a *naval*, a scoundrel, a charlatan under the guise of observing the Torah. I am tempted to ask which is worse: to designate a person as a sinner for violating one of the thirty-nine *melakhot*, or as a *naval*, one who misconstrues the significance of Shabbat, who fritters away the invitation that Shabbat extends to him for spiritual growth? The question of course is rhetorical. Someone who writes on Shabbat violates one of the thirty-nine *melakhot*

---

27. אסרו חכמים לטלטל מקצת דברים בשבת כדרך שהוא עושה בחול. ומפני מה נגעו באיסור זה? אמרו: ומה אם הזהירו נביאים וצוו שלא יהיה הילוכך בשבת כהילוכך בחול ולא **שיחת השבת כשיחת החול**, שנאמר וְדַבֵּר דָּבָר, קל וחומר שלא יהיה טלטול בשבת כטלטול בחול, **כדי שלא יהיה כיום חול בעיניו** (**משנה תורה** הלכות שבת כד, יב).

28. והענין, כי התורה הזהירה בעריות ובמאכלים האסורים, והתירה הביאה איש באשתו ואכילת הבשר והיין. א״כ ימצא בעל התאוה מקום להיות שטוף בזמת אשתו או נשיו הרבות, ולהיות בסובאי יין בזוללי בשר למו, וידבר כרצונו בכל הנבלות, שלא הוזכר איסור זה בתורה, והנה **יהיה נבל ברשות התורה** (רמב״ן, ויקרא יט, ב).

but is not called a *naval*; a *naval* is one who totally misses the point of Shabbat. He may refrain from writing on Shabbat, but he does not begin to understand what Shabbat is all about. The *naval*, the scoundrel under the guise of observing the Torah, as the Ramban uses it, is reminiscent of the phrase at the end of Devarim, *am naval velo ḥakham,*[29] particularly as the Targum understands it: "a people who indeed received the Torah but did not grow wise even with it." The Torah, as it were, was wasted on them. This, I believe, is what led the Ramban to his famous resounding phrase *naval bireshut hatorah,* a scoundrel who outwardly says, "I have a relation to the Torah," but the Torah leaves no impact on him, does not transform him at all.

SILENCE AS A FENCE AROUND WISDOM

Another example of *seyag* in the expansive, enhancing sense is the Mishnah in Avot, *seyag laḥokhmah shtikah.*[30] We shall translate it temporarily as "silence is a fence around wisdom." What does that mean?

There are two startling halakhot of the Rambam in *Hilkhot De'ot,* chapter 2, halakhot 4 and 5. In halakhah 4, the Rambam says:

> One should consistently maximize silence (*shtikah*), speaking only of wisdom or what needs to be said to sustain the body. It was said of Rav, the student of Rabbeinu Hakadosh, that he never in all his days engaged in idle conversation – which characterizes most people's conversations. Even in [procuring one's] bodily necessities one should not talk too much. The Sages counseled this, saying: "Whoever talks too much brings sin"; and they said: "Regarding the [business of the] body, I have found nothing but silence to be good." Similarly, in discussing Torah or wisdom, a scholar's words should be few, but rich in meaning. That is the

29. עַם נָבָל וְלֹא חָכָם (דברים לב, ו); עמא דקבילו אורייתא ולא חכימו. (תרגום אונקלוס)

30. "סְיָג לחכמה שתיקה" (אבות ג, יג); עיינו גם אבות א, יז: "לא מצאתי לגוף טוב אלא שתיקה... כל המרבה בדברים מביא חטא".

> import of the Sages' admonition "One should always teach one's students with verbal economy."[31]

Even in areas where you are not only permitted, but commanded to talk, to engage in speaking about Torah and wisdom, your talk should be measured. You should refrain from idle talk; *shtikah* here is close to silence, but it is not complete silence. When you have something to say relating to wisdom, relating to Torah, then share it with others. However, our model should be Rav, the student of R. Yehudah Hanasi who never engaged in idle talk; the Rambam adds to this nonchalantly that idle talk is the conversation of most people. Use a minimum of words, only that which is necessary to express an idea. The *ideas* should be abundant; the *words* as sparse as possible. Take note of the Rambam's emphasis: "One should always teach one's students with verbal economy."[32] When one teaches, say only what is necessary and not more.

Then, in halakhah 5, after his lengthy discussion about the virtue and importance of silence, the Rambam begins another halakhah concerning silence.

> Silence is a hedge round wisdom. So [a scholar] should not respond hastily [to questions] or be prolix [in his expositions]. He should teach [his] students softly and with finesse – no vociferation, no verbiage.[33]

---

31. לעולם ירבה אדם בשתיקה, ולא ידבר אלא או בדבר חכמה או בדברים שצריך להם לחיי גופו; אמרו על רב, תלמיד רבינו הקדוש, שלא שח שיחה בטלה כל ימיו, וזהו שיחת רוב כל אדם. ואפילו בצרכי הגוף לא ירבה אדם דברים. ועל זה צוו חכמים ואמרו: כל המרבה דברים – מביא חטא; ואמרו: לא מצאתי לגוף טוב אלא שתיקה. וכן בדברי תורה ובדברי חכמה, יהיו דברי האדם מעטים ועניניהם מרובים. והוא שצוו חכמים ואמרו: לעולם ישנה אדם לתלמידיו דרך קצרה (**משנה תורה** הלכות דעות ב, ד). עיינו גם הלכות טומאת צרעת, טז, י, שכתב הרמב"ם – "אבל שיחת כשרי ישראל אינה אלא בדברי תורה וחכמה".
32. על פי הגמרא: אמר רב הונא אמר רב משום רבי מאיר: לעולם ישנה אדם לתלמידו דרך קצרה (פסחים ג, ב).

    This is not only in the context of teaching. It is (1) a general rule of speech, and (2) it applies to prayer as well: "Therefore let your words be few" (Kohelet 5:1).
33. סְיָג לחכמה שתיקה, לפיכך לא ימהר להשיב ולא ירבה לדבר, וילמד לתלמידים בשובה ונחת בלא צעקה ובלא אריכות לשון (**משנה תורה** הלכות דעות ב, ה).

What is the relationship between these two halakhot? What is the nature of the silence in halakhah 5? In this halakhah, which opens with *seyag laḥokhmah shtikah,* silence actually defines wisdom; it is not something extraneous at all. You cannot use the image of a fence or hedge, which is extraneous, which creates distance between the fence and that which is being protected. Silence here refers to the way you talk, to the mode of speech, to the structure of speech, to the effectiveness and impact of speech. It regulates its expression and maximizes its effectiveness. It sees to it that the content and the form of wisdom are commensurate.[34]

Clearly, there are two types of silence. Halakhah 4 presents one type of silence: "One should consistently maximize silence, speaking only of wisdom," that is to say, minimize your abuse of this special gift from God.[35] But halakhah 5 tells us how to cultivate a careful, constructive speech, a meticulous, measured, terse, and thoughtful language that will help us achieve the impact that the words are supposed to have.[36]

There is thus a remarkable parallel to our analysis above in the context of Shabbat. Here too, Ramban's comments are cogent. In the Ramban's discussion of "the scoundrel under the guise of observing the Torah," he warns that "one should guard his mouth and his tongue from

34. אבל המצווה והרצוי, אם יוכל האדם לדבר בהם כל ימי חייו הרי זו היא התכלית, אלא שהוא צריך עם זה שני דברים, האחד שיהו מעשיו מתאימים לדברים כמו שאומרים נאים דברים היוצאים מפי עושיהם... וחכמים אומרים לחסיד המלמד את המדות הנעלות, דרוש ולך נאה לדרוש. ואמר הנביא רַנְּנוּ צַדִּיקִים בַּה׳ לַיְשָׁרִים נָאוָה תְהִלָּה. והענין השני הוא הקצור, שישתדל להרבות את הענינים בדברים מעטים לא שיהא הדבר להפך, והוא אמרם לעולם ישנה אדם לתלמידיו דרך קצרה (רמב״ם, פירוש למסכת אבות, פרק א׳ משנה טז).

According to this, there are two requirements for speech: (1) consistency – there must be a carryover from word to deed, and (2) brevity – needless talk is abuse of language.

35. The Rambam in *Moreh Nevukhim,* 3:8, refers to speech as a gracious gift from God. If you are careful in spending money, you should certainly be careful in your speech.

36. המאירי הציע פירוש דומה לזה של הרמב״ם בדגשים דומים בפירושו לאבות על ״עשו סיג לתורה״: ״שהוא הזהיר להיות כל אדם שומר פיו לעשות גדר לדבריו, ולתת להם גבול לבל יכביד השומעים בהם. וכ״ש שכשמדבר בדברי תורה שלא ידבר בהן אלא בזמן הראוי, ובשיעור הראוי, ובמקום הראוי לו, ובדברים הראויים לו, אם מצדו אם מצד השומעים. ובמשלי הערב אמרו על חכם אחד שהיה מאריך בדבריו יותר מדאי ושאלו לו: ׳מדוע אתה עובר הגבול להאריך כל כך. אמר להם: מפני שיבינו הפתאים. אמרו לו: בעבור שהפתאים יבינו המשכילים יקוצו״ (**בית הבחירה לרבינו מנחם המאירי, מסכת אבות** עם מבוא הערות וביאורים מאת שלמה זלמן הבלין, מכון אופק תשנ״ה), עמ׳ 8.

becoming polluted with excessive, gluttonous eating or from unseemly speech."[37]

The two are equal: extreme gluttony or epicurean behavior in matters of food, and defilement of speech, that gracious gift which must be used carefully and thoughtfully. The Rambam's two-tiered interpretation of "silence is a hedge around wisdom" teaches us this positive aspect of *seyag* and prevents one from becoming a "scoundrel under the guise of observing the Torah."

It should be self-evident that in order to know what kinds of *seyag* are necessary and constructive, one must have a clear, authentic perception of Torah, one must know its objectives and its ideals; otherwise *seyag* will be irrelevant or trivial, and misleading. The power and profundity, the challenge and enchantment of the *masorah* must be known. Its details must be correctly perceived and analyzed, and each detail must mesh harmoniously with the total structure of Torah.

The Gemara in Gittin presents two opinions concerning the giving of the Torah. One is that the Torah was originally given scroll by scroll; the second is that the Torah was given as a complete book.[38] We can interpret the two opinions to reflect on the nature of Torah. It is composed of many details, scroll by scroll, but at the same time Torah must be viewed in its totality, as a complete book. In order to fulfill the mandate to "make a fence around the Torah," we need to view Torah in its totality. We need to ascertain the goals, the values, and the ideals of the Torah; we need to relate the details to the totality and then make sure that the totality is reflected in the details.

SUPER-CATEGORIES

Kedushah, Holiness

How does one achieve this knowledge of Torah? How are we to gain that insight that will help every person to develop his own *seyag*,

---

37. ישמור פיו ולשונו מהתגאל בִרבוי האכילה הגסה ומן הדבור הנמאס. (רמב"ן, ויקרא יט, ב)

38. תורה מגילה מגילה ניתנה... תורה חתומה ניתנה. (גיטין ס, א)

as it says in *Avot Derabbi Natan,* that every individual "should make a *seyag* around his words"?[39]

One approach, probably the most fruitful one, is to look for certain overarching principles or super-categories. If you can identify and analyze some of these, then you can understand the function and purpose of *seyag*. For example, the Rambam in *Sefer Hamitzvot,* principle 4, lists a number of commandments that are not to be included in the 613 scripturally mandated commandments, because they encompass the entire Torah; they are applicable to all mitzvot. These are the overarching principles, the super-categories. One of the examples he cites is "You shall keep My charge," the verse with which we started.[40] That is not counted as a positive commandment because it includes everything. Every mitzvah is subject to, or can be related to, this.

The example which vexes him most is "You shall be holy" (Vayikra 19:2):

> Many have also erred concerning this root principle and have counted "You shall be holy" as one of the positive commandments…and were not aware that "You shall be holy" is one of the commands to observe the entire Torah. The meaning of the verse is to be holy through observing all of the positive commands and abstaining from all the negative commands.[41]

Kedushah, holiness, is a goal of the entire Torah; it is not just a single mitzvah. It is inherent in every mitzvah and is also a prerequisite for each mitzvah. It can be defined in many different ways; here is one example:

Kedushah means purposiveness, a heightened awareness of the meaning of time and, as a result, the proper utilization of time. Nothing

---

39. עשה סיג **לדבריך** כדרך שעשה הקדוש ברוך הוא סיג לדבריו (**אבות דרבי נתן** הוספה ב, נוסחא א, פרק א).

40. וּשְׁמַרְתֶּם אֶת מִשְׁמַרְתִּי (ויקרא יח, ל). See at n. 2 above.

41. וּשְׁמַרְתֶּם אֶת מִשְׁמַרְתִּי ורבים כאלו, וכבר טעו בשורש הזה גם כן עד שמנו קדושים תהיו מצוה מכלל מצוות עשה. ולא ידעו שאמרו קְדֹשִׁים תִּהְיוּ, וְהִתְקַדִּשְׁתֶּם וִהְיִיתֶם קְדֹשִׁים הם ציווין לקיים כל התורה כאילו יאמר היה קדוש בעשותך כל מה שצויתיך ונזהר מכל מה שהזהרתיך ממנו (רמב"ם, **ספר המצוות,** שורש ד).

is random or routine; *kedushah* negates meaninglessness and lawlessness. It endows one with sensitivity to the meaning and importance of routine.

At the end of Devarim God says to Moshe and Aharon that they are going to die, "because you betrayed Me (*me'altem)* in the midst of the Israelites" and then "because you did not sanctify Me (*lo kidashtem)* in the midst of the Israelites."[42] How many sins are we dealing with? One or two? Are *me'altem* and *lo kidashtem,* synonymous? *Me'ilah* is a specific transgression which can be defined very precisely. What is *lo kidashtem oti ,* "you did not sanctify Me"?

R. Meir Simḥah, in his work *Meshekh Ḥokhmah,* utilizes the Gra's definition of *din veḥeshbon; din* refers to specific actions, *ḥeshbon* to opportunity wasted, time that one did not use properly.[43] *Lo kidashtem* means Moshe and Aharon missed an irretrievable chance to accomplish something great. *Kedushah,* therefore, is to act creatively and constructively in implementing the will of God. "Because you betrayed Me (*me'altem bi),*" you did not do what you were supposed to do; that is *me'ilah,* you didn't follow My commandment. But perhaps even more important, *Al asher lo kidashtem oti,* you missed an opportunity to spread and illustrate *kedushah.* This is a beautiful, stunning interpretation of R. Meir Simḥah! I cite it to support what I say, that *kedushah* means purposiveness, a sense of the importance of time and of opportunity.

In spreading *kedushah* one must attain the right balance between involvement and withdrawal. One is neither enslaved to or by society, nor is one hostile to it. It means doing everything, being involved in mundane activities, contributing to a just society, but never blurring the focus or losing sight of the goal, as implied in the following interpretation by the Ḥatam Sofer. He cites the verse in Shemot: "and all the people in whose midst you are, shall see how awesome are the LORD's deeds which I will perform for you."[44] The Ḥatam Sofer explains that

---

42. עַל אֲשֶׁר מְעַלְתֶּם בִּי בְּתוֹךְ בְּנֵי יִשְׂרָאֵל... עַל אֲשֶׁר לֹא קִדַּשְׁתֶּם אוֹתִי בְּתוֹךְ בְּנֵי יִשְׂרָאֵל (דברים לב, נא).

43. "עַל אֲשֶׁר מְעַלְתֶּם", זה בחינת "דין" – על אשר מעלו. "עַל אֲשֶׁר לֹא קִדַּשְׁתֶּם אוֹתִי" – זה בחינת "חשבון" מה שהיו יכולים לקדש שמו יתברך (ר' מאיר שמחה הכהן, **משך חכמה** דברים לב, נא).

44. וְרָאָה כָל הָעָם אֲשֶׁר אַתָּה בְקִרְבּוֹ אֶת מַעֲשֵׂה ה' כִּי נוֹרָא הוּא אֲשֶׁר אֲנִי עֹשֶׂה עִמָּךְ (שמות לד, י); כותב החתם סופר: "וזה וְלֹא קָם נָבִיא עוֹד בְּיִשְׂרָאֵל, להיות בישראל באמצעם ומעורב ביניהם,

the Children of Israel were aware that Moshe Rabbeinu was "in their midst"; he led them, he fought their battles, and he adjudicated their disputes. But at the same moment they realized that this is the Moshe Rabbeinu that also has risen to the greatest spiritual heights and has, as it were, spoken to God "face-to-face." They will thus understand that if such a person can also be "in their midst," the conclusion must be "how awesome are the LORD's deeds."

In a similar vein, the Netziv says in his commentary on the verse in Devarim, "The LORD will establish you as His holy people, as He swore to you, if you keep the commandments of the LORD your God," that even when engaged in fulfilling mitzvot in one's daily affairs, one should aspire to *kedushah* and *devekut*.[45]

Temimut, Perfection

Another example of a super-category is *temimut*, perfection. The Ramban at the end of his critical comments on *Sefer Hamitzvot* lists a number of mitzvot which he says escaped the Rambam completely. One of them (mitzvah 8) is "You must be wholehearted or perfect, *tamim*, with the LORD your God."[46] This is the mitzvah of *temimut*, of which he says: "The subject of this command is that we commit ourselves solely to God, blessed be He, and believe that He alone governs all."[47]

For the Ramban, *temimut* means total belief, unqualified trust in God, refraining from looking for signs or trying to guess the future.

ולא בהתבודדות מהם ׳כמשה׳ כאשר היה משה. כי היה מלכם ועשה מלחמותיהם ודנם ושפט אותם, ובכל זאת אֲשֶׁר יְדָעוֹ ה׳ פָּנִים אֶל פָּנִים, אספקלריא המאירה שהיא המדרגה היותר גדולה. ובזה יש לפרש הפסוק וְרָאָה כָל הָעָם אֲשֶׁר אַתָּה בְקִרְבּוֹ, שאתה ביניהם תמיד, עי״ז יראו ויבינו את מעשה ה׳ כי נורא״ (חת״ם סופר, **תורת משה** ספר שמות, פרשת כי תשא, מכון חתם סופר תשס״ה, דף פז, ב).

45. יְקִימְךָ ה׳ לוֹ לְעַם קָדוֹשׁ כַּאֲשֶׁר נִשְׁבַּע לָךְ כִּי תִשְׁמֹר אֶת מִצְוֹת ה׳ אֱלֹקֶיךָ (דברים כח, ט). כותב על זה הנצי״ב: ״כי תשמור וגו׳. באופן שמי שרוצה להתנהג בקדושה ודביקות לא יחפוץ להיבדל ממעשה המצוות, שלפעמים הם מסירים הדבקות. אבל מכל מקום הכרח לשמור המצוות בין השייכים לשמים בין השייכים לאדם וחברו״ (**העמק דבר** שם).

46. תָּמִים תִּהְיֶה עִם ה׳ אֱלֹקֶיךָ. (דברים יח, יג)

47. וענין הצוואה הזאת שנייחד לבבנו אליו לבדו יתברך, ושנאמין שהוא לבדו עושה כל, והוא היודע אמתת כל עתיד, וממנו לבדו נדרוש הבאות מנביאיו או מאנשי חסידיו (**ספר המצוות לרמב״ם עם השגות הרמב״ן** [למעלה עמ׳ 31, הערה 45], מצוות ששכח אותן הרב ממצות עשה, מצוה שמינית עמ׳ רמח).

What is striking is that at the end of his long exposition he speculates as to why the Rambam did not include this mitzvah in his list. His speculation is right on target:

> Perhaps the Rambam considered this command as one that encompasses all the mitzvot, instructing us to walk in the ways of the Torah, as it is written, "Happy are those whose way is perfect (*temimei derekh*), who follow the teaching of the LORD" (Tehillim 119:1), and for this reason he did not count it as a specific mitzvah.[48]

"*Perhaps*," says the Ramban, but with his permission I would say *certainly* the Rambam thought that *tamim tihyeh* was a super-category that relates to the entire Torah. I'm really puzzled why the Ramban is so tentative. He could very well have substantiated his position by citing the Rambam himself. In fact, the Rambam in *Hilkhot Avodah Zarah* defines *tamim tihyeh* very differently than does the Ramban. The Rambam states:

> Whoever believes in these [magical practices] and their like, thinking them valid and scientific yet forbidden by the Torah, is but one of the ignorant and intellectually deficient, of a class with women and children, whose intellects are incomplete; whereas masters of wisdom and the intellectually perfect know through irrefutable proofs that none of those things forbidden by the Torah is science. They are but vanity and inanity into which the intellectually deficient [people of antiquity] let themselves be drawn, and on whose account they forsook all the paths of truth. It is for this reason that the Torah, when proscribing all of those inanities, said: "You shall be wholehearted (*tamim tihyeh*) with the LORD your God" (Devarim 18:13).[49]

---

48. ואולי הרב חשב שהיא צוואה כוללת המצוות כולן ללכת בדרכי התורה, כענין שנאמר אַשְׁרֵי תְמִימֵי דָרֶךְ הַהֹלְכִים בְּתוֹרַת ה׳ ולכן לא הביאה בחשבונו (שם).

49. כל המאמין בדברים האלו וכיוצא בהן, ומחשב בלבו שהן אמת ודבר חכמה אבל התורה אסרתן – אינן אלא מן הסכלים ומחסרי הדעת, ובכלל הנשים והקטנים שאין דעתן שלימה. אבל בעלי החכמה ותמימי הדעת ידעו בראיות ברורות שכל אלו הדברים שאסרה תורה אינם דברי חכמה אלא תהו והבל שנמשכו בהן חסרי הדעת ונטשו כל דרכי האמת בגללן. ומפני זה אמרה תורה

Thus, the Ramban's intuition was completely correct that for the Rambam *tamim tihyeh* was a principle applying to the entire Torah. It impacts upon the contours and the content of every mitzvah in a fashion similar to the way that for Reb Ḥayyim Volozhiner, in his commentary on Avot,[50] the mitzvah of fear of God, *yir'ah,* is not just a single mitzvah, but rather flavors every mitzvah. Similarly, the Rambam in *Hilkhot Avodah Zarah* says that *tamim tihyeh* affects, flavors, and determines the significance of every single mitzvah. *Tamim tihyeh im Hashem* means that observance is accompanied by commitment and insight; it is congruent with one's mind and heart. There should be a clear intellectual conviction which accompanies the meticulous performance of mitzvot.

Tamim tihyeh thus tells us two things according to the Rambam: Do not approach the Torah in an intellectually undisciplined way, in a religiously insensitive way;[51] and, more specifically, the essence of *temimut* is not to say that the intellect and Torah have nothing in common. There is a popular position today that piety can be nurtured only by some kind of obscurantism.[52] For the Rambam, *tamim tihyeh* is a repudiation of the claim that there must be a separation of piety from intellectual ability.[53]

Tamim tihyeh is similar to other precepts such as *kedoshim tihyu,* you should be holy, which the Rambam also did not count as a mitzvah as they are both super-categories. *Vehalakhta bidrakhav,* you shall walk in His ways,[54] although counted as a mitzvah, also has the character of a super-category.

כשהזהירה על כל אלו ההבלים: תָּמִים תִּהְיֶה עִם ה׳ אֱלֹקֶיךָ (**משנה תורה** הלכות עבודה זרה יא, טז).

50. ר׳ חיים מוולוז׳ין, **רוח חיים** על מסכת אבות, תשנ״ד, פרק א׳ משנה א׳, עמ׳ לה

51. This is a common theme in the Rambam.

52. See the author's "Religion and Law," in Isadore Twersky, *Studies in Jewish Law and Philosophy* (Ktav, 1982), 212, n. 6.

53. There are only two mitzvot that one does *im Hashem,* with God, which implies a command, as opposed to *lifnei Hashem,* before God. The two mitzvot are *tamim tihyeh im Hashem* as we see here (above, n. 46), and *hatzneah lekhet im Hashem,* "walking humbly with God" (Mikhah 6:8). [In both of these examples, we are not dealing with an explicit imperative that creates one of the 613 mitzvot, but rather a mode of behavior that it is applicable to all mitzvot.]

54. Devarim 28:9. Cf. chapter 1, first section, for uses of this verse.

With respect to the latter, "walking in His ways" relates not only to specific acts of *ḥesed,* kindness; it is character perfection as well. Paraphrasing the words of the Rov:

> The moral imperative of *vehalakhta bidrakhav,* you shall walk in His ways, releases creative, spiritual energies in the individual who realizes the impossibility of achieving *devekut,* cleaving to God, and consequently, imitation of God is exhilarating. It is a mitzvah and nevertheless triggers individuality, spirituality and creativity.[55]
>
> Creativity is not only writing, sculpturing and composing, but is also self-realization in the context of Torah norms and letting one's potential reach fruition.[56]

Similarly, we should view all *ta'amei hamitzvot* from the perspective of super-categories. To be aware of the goal of the mitzvah has a determining influence on how you perform the mitzvah. Even with respect to *ḥukkim* one must show that they are sources of *temimut, kedushah,* or *Vehalakhta bidrakhav.* The Gemara in Berakhot 47b asks: "How does one define an *am ha'aretz*?" The upshot of the Gemara is that an *am ha'aretz* is one who lacks perspective, lacks cognizance of goals, lacks a sense of spirituality, and lacks yearning for God.

The Rambam's definition of *mezuzah* is a superb illustration of how awareness of the goal of the mitzvah has a determining influence on how you perform it. The Rambam says in *Hilkhot Tefillin Umezuzah Vesefer Torah* that *mezuzah* is not a protection, not an amulet, but a reminder of the unity of God.[57] If one does not know that this is the essence of the mitzvah, there is no way one can perform it.

---

55. Based on Rabbi Joseph B. Soloveitchik, *And from There You Shall Seek* (p. 25, n. 30), 75–76.
56. Based on Rabbi Joseph B. Soloveitchik, *Halakhic Man,* translated from the Hebrew by Lawrence Kaplan (Jewish Publication Society, 1983), 132.
57. מנהג פשוט שכותבים על המזוזה מבחוץ כנגד הריוח שבין פרשה לפרשה "ש־די"; ואין בזה הפסד, לפי שהוא מבחוץ. אבל אלו שכותבין מבפנים שמות המלאכים או שמות קדושים או פסוק או חותמות – הרי הן בכלל מי שאין להם חלק לעולם הבא; שאלו הטפשים, לא די להם שבטלו המצוה, **אלא שעשו מצוה גדולה שהיא יחוד השם של הקדוש ברוך הוא ואהבתו**

Here you see that *ta'amei hamitzvot* are integral and indispensable; they are not just an intellectual exercise, not something extraneous to performance, to religious life. *Ta'amei hamitzvot* constitute a kind of super-category for determining the goals, values, and norms of the Torah.

Birkhot Hatorah, Blessings of the Torah

A further illustration of our theme of overarching categories is to be found in the *birkhot hatorah,* the blessings said before the study of Torah. *Birkhot hatorah* reflect the unique status of our endless commitment to study and its purposes. The Ramban, in his additions to the Rambam's *Sefer Hamitzvot,* claims that the Rambam forgot to count *birkhot hatorah* as one of the mitzvot.[58] On the face of it he is correct. Even the commentary *Megillat Esther* on *Sefer Hamitzvot,* which defends the Rambam at every step, says that here the Ramban is correct.

However, irrespective of whether *birkhot hatorah* are scripturally or rabbinically prescribed, they clearly have special status unlike other blessings for mitzvot. The Gemara in Berakhot states:

> R. Yehudah said in the name of Shmuel: One who arose to study and has not yet recited the *Shema* must recite the blessings (for the study of Torah).[59]

R. Akiva Eiger, in his *Gilyon Hashas,* commenting on a Tosafot, states:

> The absence of a blessing that precedes a mitzvah does not preclude the performance of a mitzvah; however, the blessing before deriving pleasure from eating is preclusive.[60]

ועבודתו, כאילו הוא קמיע של הניית עצמן, כמו שעלה על לבם הסכל, שזהו דבר המהנה בהבלי העולם (**משנה תורה** הלכות תפילין ומזוזה וספר תורה ה, ד).

58. מצוה טו: שנצטוינו להודות לשמו ית' בכל עת שנקרא בתורה, על הטובה הגדולה שעשה לנו בתתו תורתו אלינו, והודיענו המעשים הרצויים לפניו שבהם ננחל חיי העולם הבא ... (**ספר המצוות לרמב"ם עם השגות הרמב"ן** [למעלה עמ' 31, הערה 45], שכחת העשין).

59. אמר רב יהודה אמר שמואל: השכים לשנות עד שלא קרא קריאת שמע צריך לברך (ברכות יא, ב).

60. דלא שייך כן אלא בברכת המצות, דהברכות אינן מעכבות. אבל בברכת הנהנין אסור לאכול בלא ברכה (ר' עקיבא איגר, **גליון הש"ס**, ברכות יב, א על התוספות ד"ה לא לאתויי נהמא).

R. Akiva Eiger is saying that according to Tosafot there is a basic difference between *birkhot hanehenin*, blessings on pleasures, and all *birkhot hamitzvot*. Regarding the former, if you fail to recite the blessing you violate a halakhah. If you eat an apple, if you take a glass of water, without reciting a *berakhah*, you have violated a halakhah. This is not so regarding *birkhot hamitzvot*. There is no such relationship between saying the *berakhah* and doing the mitzvah.

R. Ḥayyim Brisker emphasized that contrary to R. Akiva Eiger's explanation of the Tosafot, the Rambam equates *birkhot hamitzvot* and *birkhot hanehenin*:

> Just as blessings are recited before partaking of material enjoyments, similarly blessings are recited before fulfilling a mitzvah.[61]

However, *birkhot hatorah* have a special status. That is what the Gemara in Berakhot cited above emphasizes: "R. Yehudah said in the name of Shmuel that before one engages in *talmud Torah*, blessings must be recited." This is so regardless of whether this would be the requirement before engaging in every mitzvah, as the Rambam would have it, or whether every mitzvah should preferably, but not indispensably, be preceded by a *berakhah*, like R. Akiva Eiger. According to either opinion a person must recite *birkhot hatorah* before engaging in *talmud Torah*. So regardless of whether or not *birkhot hatorah* are scripturally required, they have special status.

What is unique about *birkhot hatorah*? What do we say, what do we affirm? The answer is twofold:

1. The source of Torah, the origin, the *etiology* of Torah
2. The purpose of Torah, the goal of the Torah, the *teleology* of Torah

The third *berakhah*, *venatan lanu et torato*, "He has given us His Torah," relates to the *origin* of the Torah. The *purpose* of Torah is expressed in the first two *berakhot*: *la'asok bedivrei Torah*, "to preoccupy oneself with the words of Torah," and *veha'arev na*, "Make the words of Your Torah

61. וכשם שמברכין על ההנייה, כך מברכין על כל מצוה ומצוה. (**משנה תורה** הלכות ברכות א, ג)

sweet." These two *berakhot* give direction and substance to all the individual mitzvot. The combined double purpose of Torah is, thus, the contemplative *yod'ei shemekha,* to "know Your name," and the practical, to "study Your Torah for its own sake."

This clear orientation and unmistakable objective of Torah, which grant its *berakhot* special status, is presumably the background for a startlingly new interpretation of *birkhot hatorah* by Reb Ḥayyim Brisker.[62] *Birkhot hatorah* are not *birkhot hamitzvah* but *birkhot hashevaḥ, berakhot* expressing praise.[63]

This would explain, even according to the opinion of R. Akiva Eiger and Tosafot, why the Gemara emphasizes the indispensable requirement to recite them. When one deals with Torah, one has to acknowledge our special gratitude to God; they are not *birkhot hamitzvah* that permit one to do the mitzvah, but rather *birkhot shevaḥ vehodayah* which expresses praise for the privilege of receiving the Torah and being able to study it. This accounts for the unique status of *birkhot hatorah* and why they are not listed as a scriptural mitzvah according to the Rambam. *Birkhot hatorah* are thus another example of a super-category that enables us to appreciate the overarching goals of Torah.

MINHAG, CUSTOM

We began by noting that the Rambam in *Hilkhot Mamrim* added the term *minhagot* in his delineation of *seyag.*[64] We then concretized this category by looking at how one experiences Shabbat, and at the concept of *shetikah,* and suggested that overarching super-categories such as *kedushah, temimut,* and the values inherent in *birkhot hatorah* will help one develop the intuition to identify and implement appropriate *minhagot.*

62. See *Ḥiddushei Maran Hariz Halevi al HaRambam* (Jerusalem, 5748) on *Hilkhot Berakhot,* p. 10. He quotes his father to the effect that *birkat hatorah* is not a conventional *birkat hamitzvah*: ושמעתי מפי אאמו״ר הגאון החסיד זצוקללה״ה שאמר: דברכת התורה אין הברכה על קיום המצוה של תלמוד תורה, רק דהוא דין בפני עצמו דתורה בעי ברכה.

63. This is found independently in the *Minḥat Ḥinukh*: מן התורה לומר לפי צחות הלשון... איזה שבח על נתינת התורה הקדושה (**מנחת חינוך** כרך שלישי, מכון ירושלים תשנ״א, מצוה ת״ל, עמוד קס״ו, אות קטן ה). This new interpretation of *birkat hatorah* seems to have emerged simultaneously in different parts of Europe.

64. See n. 8 above.

We are now able to approach the concept and reality of *seyag* from a new vantage point. *Seyag* is what R. Baḥya ibn Pakuda calls "duties of the heart" and "duties arrived at by rational thought,"[65] or what *Sefer Ḥasidim* refers to as "piety…which entails going beyond the explicit demands of the law," "(the use of) stratagems to achieve fear of Heaven," and "seeking the will of the Creator."[66]

One should extend the realms of religious obligation and performance in a carefully calibrated way, in a way that reflects the values and ideals of Torah. This extension, which is quite dramatic, moves not only on the perimeters of mitzvot, on the margins of religious life, but reaches to the heart of mitzvot. Indeed, that is the meaning of "beyond the letter of the law" – an inner-directed gesture, not an outer-directed one.

This understanding of *seyag* that I have tried to suggest provides, I think, the best and the most authentic way to approach and to conceptualize the entire realm of *minhag*, custom. *Minhag* is to be seen as an expansive, enhancing movement. *Minhag Yisrael Torah*[67] entails a challenge to understand and to identify the anchor of every *minhag* in Torah. Although *minhag* does not have anything to do with the issue of "neither add to it nor subtract from it,"[68] it is rooted in and relates to mitzvot. *Minhag* is not just a restrictive, protective effort to safeguard a mitzvah, but serves to enhance it. Singing *zemirot* on Shabbat and other *minhagim* of this kind are expressions of religious yearning, expressions of one's understanding of the goals and principles of the Torah; that is the context from which they emerge.

Actually, one must differentiate between the *minhagim* being discussed here and *minhagim* that reflect different interpretations of Halakhah. For example, whether one says *Aleinu leshabe'aḥ* before or

65. רבנו בחיי אבן פקודא, **ספר חובות הלבבות**. למונח "חובות הלבבות" עיינו הקדמה; למונח "מצוות שכליות" עיינו שער י' אהבת השם פרק ז.

66. "חסידות", "ערום ביראה", "רצון הבורא". עיינו **ספר חסידים** (מהדורת ראובן מרגליות, מוסד הרב קוק תשס"ז) סי' יא, עמ' סב: "וזה שורש **החסידות** שצריך לעשות לפנים משורת הדין בכל דבר שנאמר **וְחָסִיד** בְּכָל מַעֲשָׂיו"; "ויהיה אדם **ערום ביראה** ובדעת לחשוב מחשבות ערומות לתקנת העולם ולכבוד שמים" (שם, סי' יג עמ' סד); "לעשות **רצון הבורא** ולזכות את הרבים ולעשות קידוש השם ולמסור עצמו באהבת הבורא (שם, סימן ש, עמ' רמ).

67. See Tosafot, Menahot 20b.

68. לֹא תֹסֵף עָלָיו וְלֹא תִגְרַע מִמֶּנּוּ. (דברים יג, א)

after the *Shir shel Yom* and *Ein Kelokeinu* is dependent on different interpretations regarding the function of *Aleinu*. When we speak of *minhag Ashkenaz and minhag Sefard,* those *minhagim* are usually the result of differences in interpretation of Halakhah. Another example is whether or not one eats *kneidlakh* on Pesaḥ which depends on different understandings of matzah on Pesaḥ. Whether to stand during the recitation of *Kaddish* also depends on the understanding of Halakhah.

However, the *minhagim* that are expressions of religious yearning are essentially uniform and universal, not subject to differing opinions. The saying of Tehillim at various occasions is an expression of one's religious sensitivity; that is a universal *minhag* not subject to *maḥloket,* differing opinions. The singing of *zemirot* on Shabbat is a fulfillment of *vedaber davar,* not speaking of weekday affairs,[69] through which the ambience of *kedushat Shabbat,* the sanctity of the Sabbath, can be deepened. Saying *ve'eirastikh li l'olam,* "I will betroth you to Me forever,"[70] when winding the *tefillin* around the middle finger is one more example of *minhag* that reflects religious yearning and sensitivity. Such *minhagim* fulfill what the Gemara in Berakhot 17a says: "One must always use stratagems to achieve fear of Heaven";[71] Rashi interprets: "one should cleverly use strategies to intensify his sense of the awesomeness of his creator."[72] You should do whatever possible to show your sense of fear of God, *yir'at Hashem.* It does not mean new *ḥumrot,* stricter interpretations of the Halakhah. It means that as a result of understanding the purpose and objectives of the Torah, one should be able to refine one's behavior.[73]

Asu seyag latorah, make a fence around the Torah, means to enhance the values of Torah, the ideals, norms, and aspirations of Torah which we know from a patient, probing analysis and a serious, searching study of Torah itself. Only by having this sense of what the *masorah* is can we be confident of the role and function of *seyag*. This perspective

69. See n. 13 above.

70. וְאֵרַשְׂתִּיךְ לִי לְעוֹלָם. (הושע ב, כא)

71. לעולם יהא אדם ערום ביראה (ברכות יז, א). Cf. n. 66 above.

72. להערים בכל מיני ערמה ליראת בוראו. (רש"י שם)

73. "לעולם יהא אדם ערום ביראה לדעת ולהתבונן דבר מתוך דבר, ולחדש המצאות **לעשות נחת רוח ליוצרו** בכל הדרכים שאפשר" (רמח"ל, **מסילת ישרים** פרק יט, מהדורת יוסף אביבי, מכון אופק, תשע"ד, עמ' רפו).

leads us to the conclusion that all study of Torah is for the purpose of enhancing our life of Torah, of deepening our spirituality, of enabling us to live Torah more meaningfully, and of enhancing our understanding of the nature and function of *seyag*.

My proof is a Gemara in Shabbat that is referred to indirectly by the Rambam in *Hilkhot Talmud Torah* and the *Meḥaber* in *Yoreh De'ah*;[74] so it is not just Aggadah:

> When a person will have to account for his life – he is asked a series of questions: Have you conducted business faithfully? Have you designated times for Torah study (*Kavata ittim latorah*)? Have you engaged in procreation? Have you anticipated salvation? Have you engaged in the dialectics of wisdom (*Pilpalta beḥokhmah*)? Have you inferred one matter from another (*Heivanta davar mitokh davar*)?[75]

The upshot of these six questions is: Have you lived with faith and with hope, and have you acted accordingly? The questions can be split into two groups. Three of these questions relate to study: Have you designated times for Torah study? Have you engaged in the dialectics of wisdom? Have you inferred one matter from another? These three questions reflect profound, not perfunctory, study; consistent, not intermittent, application.

What is the relation between these three? The best interpretation is given by the Rambam at the end of *Moreh Nevukhim* (3:54):

> The Sages, may their memory be blessed, mention likewise that man is required first to obtain knowledge of the Torah, then to obtain wisdom, then to know what is incumbent upon him with

74. [The Rambam (*Hilkhot Talmud Torah* 3:5) and the *Shulḥan Arukh* (246:19) quote the formulation of Gemarot in Kiddushin 40b and Sanhedrin 7a; Tosafot in each relate it to our Gemara in Shabbat.]

75. בשעה שמכניסין אדם לדין אומרים לו, נשאת ונתת באמונה? קבעת עתים לתורה? עסקת בפריה ורביה? צפית לישועה? פלפלת בחכמה? הבנת דבר מתוך דבר? (שבת לא, א).

> regard to the legal science of the Law – I mean the drawing of inferences concerning what one ought to do.[76]

The Rambam says that *Kavata ittim latorah* means: Did you appropriate the *masorah*? The second stage, *Pilpalta beḥokhmah,* means: Did you exert yourself to individualize your understanding of the tradition, to demonstrate the tradition, to understand what is *kedushah, temimut, ḥokhmah*? It is not enough to say that the Torah is concerned with these concepts; did you work out in patient detail their meaning?

The third stage, and this is the most important, *Heivanta davar mitokh davar,* did you draw practical conclusions from all your study to improve your life, to make your life more consistent and meaningful? This last stage, the most startling, does not refer to a continuation of the intellectual, analytic process but rather to the application of the learning: "then to know what is incumbent upon him by virtue of his study of the Law – I mean the drawing of inferences concerning what one ought to do"; that is, what *talmud Torah* means to *you,* how it obligates you and shapes *your* behavior.

Then the Rambam repeats:

> And this should be the order observed: The opinions in question should first be known as being received through tradition.

That is the only way one should approach Torah.

> Then they should be demonstrated; then the actions through which one's way of life may be ennobled should be precisely defined.[77]

---

76. וזכרו חכמים גם כן שהאדם נתבע בידיעת התורה תחילה, ואחר כך הוא נתבע בחכמה, ואחר כך הוא נתבע במה שראוי עליו מתלמודה של תורה, רצה לומר להוציא ממנו מה שראוי לעשות (מורה נבוכים ג, נד). The English version in the text is from *Guide for the Perplexed,* trans. Shlomo Pines (University of Chicago Press, 1963), 633–634.

77. וכן ראוי שיהיה הסדר: שייוודעו הדעות ההם תחלה על דרך קבלה, ואחר כך יתבארו במופת, ואחר כך ידוקדקו המעשים המטיבים דרכי האדם (שם).

First, one should appropriate the *masorah*; then individualize the tradition – intellectual conviction should be a companion of one's observance (i.e., *temimut*); finally, one should be meticulous in defining those actions which improve the behavior of the person. One should know what Torah is, what its ideals are. The clearer one's vision, the clearer his perception of his limitations. Intellectual modesty, which is no less important than moral modesty, demands of each one of us not only to understand concepts of *kedushah, temimut,* and *ḥokhmah* as we have noted, but demands that we draw those practical conclusions from our study that will improve our life, and make it more consistent and meaningful.

THE ROV AND MODERNITY

Knowing what Torah is, having a clear perception of its ideals, is the best guide for us as people in the modern age. Modernity is a passionate, all-consuming issue for many. I want to conclude with one theme that is reflected in the Rov's teachings and attitudes. The Rov recognized modernity; he acknowledged its problems and challenges and confronted them, but did not yield or capitulate to it.

There is a particularly poignant passage in the Rov's *hesped* for R. Ḥayyim Heller which reflects the Rov's awareness of those problems and challenges. R. Ḥayyim Heller was perhaps the Rov's closest friend; he was his teacher/friend, and he would go every week from Washington Heights to visit him in his home on the West Side of Manhattan. I'm not going to talk about R. Ḥayyim Heller now, but I just want you to hear the Rov's penetrating criticism of Modern Orthodoxy, which is a term that is so important to many.[78]

> I would visit Reb Ḥayyim Heller at his home on the West Side of Manhattan with the abundance of Jewish life, which was noisy and confused, with an abundance of *shulen, batei knesset* and other organizations, clubs and centers. When I would come to his apartment I felt as if I entered a different world, a different

78. [What follows is Rabbi Twersky's paraphrastic translation of the original Hebrew. The original Hebrew and a more precise translation appear on p. 79 and n. 39.]

> level of existence – as if I crossed a time barrier, or a space barrier, and I was able to transcend this barrier which separates two different domains: one is that of the *Shakh,* the *Taz* and the *Gra,* and the other is the domain of Modern Orthodoxy.

Why is there such a difference here between the domain of earlier generations, and the domain of Modern Orthodoxy? This is how the Rov, who was the champion of Modern Orthodoxy, characterized it:

> This is a kind of religion that is unable to sprout wings, unable to rise above the mundane – its wings have been clipped so that it cannot soar – nor does it have roots that will enable it to penetrate to the depth of the religious experience.

This revolves completely around the centrality of religious experience in the teachings, the writings, and the life of the Rov. The Rov's modernity was an enthralling, sustained attempt to probe our *masorah* so as to find untapped sources and unperceived dimensions of vitality and vibrancy which make our commitment to Torah more robust and our steady performance of mitzvot more resonant. Anyone who listened to the Rov's *derashot,* who read his writings from *Ish Hahalakhah* to *The Lonely Man of Faith,* knows that he unfailingly called attention to the pulsating inner religious life of the individual who is serious about his or her observance of mitzvot. The Rambam taught us to speak and to be aware of mitzvot of belief, mitzvot of morality, in addition to mitzvot of deeds. The Rov taught us to speak and to be mindful of mitzvot of experience, emotion, love, attitude, and perception. His own comprehensive systematic interpretation of the *masorah* yielded what appears to be a new configuration, with its salient motifs.

I think the core of this is the characterization of *seyag* as I have tried to explain it: *seyag* that enhances *ḥokhmah, kedushah, temimut,* and *halikhah bidrakhav.* These core values are the super-categories, the overarching principles of the *masorah.* They are not obtained or realized by external, sometimes artificial, patterns of behavior. A beard, for example, is not automatically a sign of *kedushah*; a black hat certainly does not on its own mean that the hat is sitting on a wise head. There is no relationship between a black hat and *ḥokhmah,* wisdom, and *temimut,* being wholehearted with God, as the Rambam understands them. Exaggerated stories are not expressions of *temimut.* One achieves this rather by disciplined intellectual activity and greater morality. *Penimiyut,* inwardness, counts, not *hitzoniyut,* external, sometimes artificial, patterns of behavior, but that which stems from the inner core. That is what the proper observance of mitzvot and the deepened study of Torah is all about.

The Gemara says concerning the verse "Wisdom cries aloud in the street" that if one studies the Torah with humility, with the attitude and modality of *tzniut,* then the Torah proclaims his merit in public.[79] There is an automatic correlation here between that which one does humbly, honestly, and sincerely (*mibifnim),* and that which is perceived (*mibaḥutz*). However, if one starts with the external, only with "Wisdom cries aloud in the street," then this has no foundation or value, and does not endure.

If the Rov's statement is to be addressed – and it is quite an indictment of and a challenge to Modern Orthodoxy – then those who value the term "Modern Orthodoxy" or see it as a meaningful slogan, as a programmatic ideological formulation, should strive to anchor it in our understanding of *asu seyag latorah.*

Seyag against intellectual hubris. *Seyag* which makes for greater moral improvement. *Seyag* for self-realization through the Torah – that is the highest form of creativity. Creativity is not only through writing or composing music or sculpturing, but through self-realization within, by and through the Torah. *Seyag* which enhances the fulfillment of mitzvot, increases their meaningfulness, and makes them resonate in one's soul and mind. This is *asu seyag latorah* as a means to not a lesser, but a greater, enhanced Torah and mitzvot.

---

79. חָכְמוֹת בַּחוּץ תָּרֹנָּה (משלי א, כ), כל העוסק בתורה מבפנים תורתו מכרזת עליו מבחוץ (מועד קטן טז, ב).

See pp. 23–25 and n. 26, for a full discussion of this theme.

הרב זצ״ל

Chapter 5

The Rov

A profile of the Rov, *zekher tzaddik livrakhah,* should include comments on his persona, his teaching, and his influence. This would have been the appropriate way to introduce him, with love and reverence, during his lifetime, and it remains appropriate for a retrospective presentation. What follows is such a three-tiered introduction; should I err, I ask that the benevolent Lord forgive me.

1.

To understand fully who this great man was and what he represented, it is necessary to recall that he was, first of all, a worthy heir of the *beit harav,*[1] that most remarkable institution of modern Jewish life – vibrant, fascinating, invigorating, ennobling. The *beit harav,* sometimes referred to as *beit hamalkhut,* the house of royalty, was a focus of Jewish creativity and rabbinic leadership in Lithuania, and eventually in all of Eastern Europe. *Beit harav* became synonymous with intensive, trailblazing

1. [*Beit harav* refers to the descendants of R. Ḥayyim of Volozhin.]

Torah scholarship, exemplary piety, and dedicated leadership. We know of many uninterrupted, spiritually aristocratic traditions in the last two or three centuries of Jewish history; it is fair to say that the *beit harav* in Lithuania is in many respects probably *sui generis*, really in a class by itself, the cradle of so much of Jewish life and learning in modern times. Rabbis of the *beit harav* were trusted mentors to countless members of the Jewish communities in Europe. People, learned and unlearned, rabbis and laymen, would refer to *beit harav "mit a tzitter,"* with deep reverence and great affection.

The Rov was, I must add, not only a worthy, luminous heir of the illustrious *beit harav*, which he frequently referred to in his lectures and *shiurim*; to this should be added the special individuating characteristics of Brisk – a simple place-name that has been transformed into a complex of values, associations, and ideals, a network of great achievements and lofty aspirations. Brisk became a code word for conceptual precision and rigor in Torah study; laser-sharp analysis of and commentary on baffling passages or difficult themes; economy of expression and clarity of exposition; intellectual honesty together with intellectual boldness, strenuous discipline, and disciplined sensitivity – all this as well as a pervasive tradition of *ḥesed*. *Rav ḥesed ve'emet*, abundant in goodness and truth, was an uplifting, enticing ideal and a remarkable, irresistible reality. Reb Ḥayyim's acts of *ḥesed* are legendary; the Rov's *ḥesed* was bountiful.

2.

The Rov was all this and more, because his glorious heritage was filtered through his unique personality, through the original constructs of his mind and heart, through that new entity formed by his majestic Torah learning together with his all-encompassing philosophic, scientific, and humanistic education. We need to be precise: even his sovereign mastery of the traditional sources of Halakhah together with his creative control of Aggadah, Kabbalah, Jewish philosophy, biblical exegesis, and the literature of Ḥasidism would make his learning unique – how much more so with the catalytic addition of the other ingredients. To be sure, comprehensiveness, impressively wide-ranging learning, was always the lodestar of *gedolei Yisrael* – it was assumed that rabbinic authorities had mastered the vast corpus of Torah teachings. However, his knowledge and range of associations in the universe of Torah and *ḥokhmah,* his erudition and creativity, his powers of analysis and interpretation, his insight and intuition represent a special kind of comprehensiveness. This needs to be recognized and underscored, for even apparently devoted students are not able to acknowledge the true dimensions of his uniqueness. As we shall note, it is easier – yet unpardonable – to reduce the extraordinary to the ordinary; this is the case even if the ordinary refers to recognized standards of intellectual-spiritual greatness. There are differences even among the great, and we need to free ourselves from routinized thinking in order to perceive and appreciate these differences. The Rambam already taught us that among the "causes of disagreement" is the fact that "man has in his nature a love of, and an inclination for, that to which he is habituated. For this reason also man is blind to the apprehension of the true realities."[2] It takes special effort and honest concentration to transcend conventions of perception and expression, to recognize something new and beautiful and authentic – something beautiful in its original mode and in its authentic force.

As for comprehensiveness, the Rov always taught that for Torah to be rich and repercussive, charming and challenging, timely and timeless, it must be comprehensive and commodious and dare not be compartmentalized or fragmented, shallow or routine. In Kiddushin our Rabbis interpret *veshinnantam levanekha,* "you shall teach them diligently to your children," strikingly: "Do not read *veshinnantam* but rather *veshilashtam.* A person should always divide his study time into three parts: a third should be devoted to Scripture (*Mikra*), a third to Mishnah, and a third to Talmud."[3] How are we to understand the transition from *veshinnantam* to *veshilashtam?* This is certainly not to be seen as just another application of the well-known *al tikrei* principle, which is based upon a different vocalization of the same letters (e.g., *banayikh-bonayikh*); phonetics and semantics are intertwined in cases of *al tikrei*

2. *Moreh Nevukhim,* 1:31. See also *Peirush Hamishnah, Sanhedrin, Perek Helek,* ed. R. Yosef Kapah, 203–204.

3. מאי דכתיב: וְשִׁנַּנְתָּם לְבָנֶיךָ (דברים ו, ז)? אל תקרי ושננתם אלא ושלשתם, לעולם ישלש אדם שנותיו, שליש במקרא, שליש במשנה, שליש בתלמוד (קידושין ל, א).

in order to focus our attention on a new insight or novel inference.[4] It appears that we have here a new conceptualization, a dynamic interpretation which underscores a basic principle and essential feature of Torah study. *Veshinnantam* means to have a clear, unobstructed grasp of the subject matter (Torah) in its entirety, which may then be transmitted without hesitation, with zeal and accuracy, charm and authoritativeness:

> That matters of Torah should be *meḥudadim befikha,* sharp and clear in your mouth, so that if a person asks you something, do not answer him with a stutter; rather, answer him immediately.[5]

This mode of teaching and transmission is attainable only if one has comprehensive scope and the ability to systematize; that is the thrust of *veshilashtam* as setting the groundwork for *veshinnantam* – study methodically so as to include everything (*Mikra,* Mishnah, Talmud [in which, according to the Rambam, philosophy is included]), and then you will be in a position to transmit Torah precisely and unfalteringly. Fragmentation often results in distortion.

At the beginning of *Hilkhot Talmud Torah,* the Rambam cites *veshinnantam* when emphasizing the obligation to teach Torah to everyone – all students are perceived as sons – whereas he could have cited the verse "and you shall teach [the words of the Torah] to your children."[6] He says:

> but not *only* his son and son's son; a commandment, rather, devolves on every Israelite scholar to teach all students, even if they are not his offspring. For [where Scripture] says, "and you shall teach them diligently to your sons," we have it on tradition: "'your sons' are your students."[7]

---

4. See pp. 27–29 for a parallel discussion.
5. ת"ר וְשִׁנַּנְתָּם שיהו דברי תורה מחודדים בפיך. שאם ישאל לך אדם דבר אל תגמגם ותאמר לו, אלא אמור לו מיד (קידושין ל, א).
6. וְלִמַּדְתֶּם אֹתָם אֶת בְּנֵיכֶם. (דברים יא, יט)
7. ולא בנו ובן בנו בלבד, אלא מצוה על כל חכם וחכם מישראל ללמד את כל התלמידים אף על פי שאינן בניו, שנאמר: וְשִׁנַּנְתָּם לְבָנֶיךָ (דברים ו, ז), מפי השמועה למדו: בניך אלו תלמידיך (**משנה תורה** הלכות תלמוד תורה א, ב).

We must be attentive to the significance of this formulation.

It appears that there are in fact two levels of teaching: *limmud* – teaching everyone something, on many different levels – a task which everyone is able to perform in one way or another; *shinun* – teaching which requires finely honed interpretive-expository skills and extensive knowledge, which only the Torah sages have acquired. This explains the Maimonidean formulation which shifts from the commandment to teach one's children and grandchildren to the obligation incumbent upon every scholar to teach all the disciples even though they are not his children. In sum, *veshinnantam,* interpreted also as *veshilashtam,* underscores the lesson that the ideal fulfillment of the mitzvah of *talmud Torah* (to study and to teach) hinges on lucid, systematic knowledge which is all-inclusive. Seen from this perspective, it is clear why *talmud Torah* is a special, open-ended mitzvah which is fulfilled with different degrees of intensity and creativity by different people.[8]

The Rov's virtuosic, versatile teaching is a vigorous, persuasive illustration of the truth of this interpretation. His Torah is comprehensive and therefore sharp; it is systematic and therefore effusive; his fulfillment of the mitzvah reflects his individuality. He occupies a position in Torah teaching which is his and his alone.

3.

What needs to be emphasized repeatedly and unequivocally is the Rov's uniqueness. His extraordinary Torah erudition together with his wide-ranging general knowledge, his dazzling brilliance, lucid, compelling analysis, phenomenal originality (which did not tolerate the shallow or the commonplace), astonishing intuition, almost legendary preoccupation with Torah (even when drinking a cup of tea or crossing the street, as was pointed out by my son Reb Mosheh), uncompromising honesty, unfailing eloquence, deep-seated sensitivity and lyricism, carefully crafted philosophy (or *hashkafah),* and overpowering charisma – all combined to shape a remarkable Torah personality, unlike any other we

8. *Mishneh Torah, Hilkhot Talmud Torah* 1:1–3 and the beautiful comments of *Or Same'aḥ.* See p. 16 at n. 11 and p. 92.

knew. This is the concept and reality of "not so My servant Moshe."[9] It is a cardinal principle that Mosaic prophecy is not only of a higher order but is intrinsically different, unique, generically and qualitatively incomparable. Failure to recognize that Moshe was not just another prophet was, in the opinion of the Rambam, the error and sin of Miriam; she did not malign or slander her brother, but she who was "older than he and had nurtured him on her knees and had put herself in jeopardy to save him," did not acknowledge his unique status and stature. "She did not slander him but erred by comparing him to all other prophets."[10] Failure to discern precisely and acknowledge properly the true greatness of a person is part of *leitzanut velashon hara,* "raillery and slander" according to the Rambam.[11]

Many years ago, the Rov mentioned to me with words of high praise an article on Reb Ḥayyim Brisker by R. Meir Berlin in which the latter used the expressive, repercussive phrase: "not so My servant Moshe" to characterize Reb Ḥayyim vis-à-vis his contemporaries – indeed truly preeminent *gedolei Yisrael,* whose light never dims. The point was that Reb Ḥayyim was unquestionably different even in this galaxy of great sages; routine praise, even if sincere, misses the mark.

The Rov subsequently used this same highly charged phrase to portray his uncle the Brisker Rov, and we may properly, with a full measure of intellectual rigor and accountability, honesty and discipline, apply it to the Rov. Let us listen to his words and learn from them:

> Nevertheless, "not so My servant Moshe"... the Brisker Rov was utterly dissimilar and completely set apart from all the scholars of his generation; different in his manner and his comportment. The description *gedol hador,* the outstanding rabbi of the generation, is inadequate and does not express his distinct characteristics.

---

9. לֹא כֵן עַבְדִּי מֹשֶׁה. (במדבר יב, ז)

10. "שהיא גדולה ממנו בשנים, וגידלתו על ברכיה, וסכנה בעצמה להצילו... והיא לא דברה בגנותו, אלא טעת, שהשוָת אותו לשאר נביאים" (**משנה תורה** הלכות טומאת צרעת טז, י).

11. "שיחת הרשעים שהוא הליצנות ולשון הרע ... דברי הבאי ... גנות הצדיקים" (**משנה תורה** שם). להספד על הרב מבריסק עיינו "מה דודך מדוד", **דברי הגות והערכה** (ההסתדרות הציונית העולמית תשמ"ב), עמ' 57–98. האפיון של משה רבינו נמצא בעמ' 65 והלאה. עיינו גם **בהלכות יסודי התורה** ז, ב.

> He was unique in his generation; he was peerless. His conceptual universe, his world outlook, his piety, moral character, and deeds cannot be captured in the platitudes of the eulogizers.... The eulogies that were delivered at his funeral and those that were written afterward placed his originality and his uniqueness in a Procrustean bed. Rather than describe the person as he really was, he became what his eulogizers, with their hackneyed verbiage, wanted him to be.[12]

What could be more appropriate for us as we continue to think about the Rov and confront the challenging and daunting task of portraying him as he was, and not as stereotyped phraseology or conventional plaudits would depict him, not as he would appear as the result of self-mirroring. We all know that language, imperfect to begin with, is debased; we find everywhere inflated rhetoric, meaningless hyperbole, sweeping generalization, unbalanced comparison, insipid stereotype, perfunctory praise. The leveling process casts its net even on truly great *ḥakhmei Yisrael*; they are presented as if they were all alike – same youthful precocity, same Torah expertise, same piety, same kind of communal leadership. In this scheme there is no room for individuating characteristics. As for us, there is no fear of contradiction in saying simply and forthrightly – without any trace of posthumous flattery or eulogistic license – that the Rov was different: different in his teaching, different in his outlook, different in his style, different in his behavior, different in his charisma. Indeed, "not so My servant Moshe."[13]

---

12. ובכל זאת, לא כן עבדי משה... הרב מבריסק הלא היה מופרד ומופרש מהם; שונה בדרכיו ואורחותיו. התואר גדול הדור אינו הולמו ואינו מבטא את האופייני לו. היחיד שבדור או בחיר הדור היה. עולמו המחשבתי, השקפתו, חסידותו, מידותיו ופעולותיו אינם נתפסים במטבעות שטבעו הספדנים... ההספדים שנאמרו אחרי מיתתו והמאמרים שנכתבו עליו קיצצו כמיטת סדום את מקוריותו וייחודו של האיש הזה. במקום להביע את אשר היה האיש, נהיה הוא את אשר רצו הספדנים לומר עליו בכליהם הלשוניים שכבר העלו חלודה ("מה דודך מדוד" [למעלה הערה 11], עמ' 69).

13. Our Rabbis affirm (Mo'ed Katan 25a) that חכם כבודו בהספדו, a sage's honor is expressed in his eulogy. What meaningful link is there between a eulogy and honor to the sage? A wise man does not need praise during his lifetime and certainly not posthumously. Apparently, our Rabbis teach that a *hesped* (eulogy), honest and sensitive, allusive and revealing, honors the departed sage by sharply delineating

The truth is that it is not really possible for anyone to say, without proper qualification, that the Rov was identical with his father and grandfather – great tribute that it is, this would be an example of a kind of oversimplification which impoverishes our spiritual-religious history. Of course, there were basic similarities and common features, but equally evident is the fact that there were essential differences and individuating features. Juxtaposing the *semikhah* given him by the Kovner Rov, R. Avraham Shapiro, and the letter written about him by his father in 1935 is a good way of balancing and integrating judicious comparison to his ancestors with candid recognition of his own persona. The Kovner Rov underscored with passionate elegance the intellectual similarities between grandfather and grandson:

> The inspiration of his grandfather, the "living great lion of the group [of *talmidei ḥakhamim* of the generation]," has rested upon him.... Like his grandfather, he has mastered the sea of the Talmud to its very depths. No difficult text baffles him, he reveals hidden meanings, deciphers the concealed, and with a piercing ray of light illuminates the meaning of obscure halakhot.[14]

The Rov's father readily and emphatically acknowledged the unique endowment of his son: his unique talents together with his unique training, his erudition coupled with his analytical skills, his mastery of Halakhah and of Jewish thought, his great creativity in the study of Torah and philosophy. The father introduces the son, whom he describes as

---

the magnitude of our indebtedness to him and the scope of his influence. Any posthumous evaluation should enrich our lives by helping us appropriate the teachings of the *ḥakham*; it must, therefore, be true and disciplined. This is how we honor the *ḥakham*: by engaging in a meditation and reflection galvanized by a spiritual-intellectual teleology. In this way, the sage remains a source and a model, a stimulus and a catalyst, a challenge and a guide. We are obligated to recognize the unique characteristics and achievements of the *ḥakham*.

14. "נחה עליו רוח זקנו הארי החי הגדול שבחבורה... כמוהו מושל בים התלמוד עד עמקי תהומותיו, וכל רז לא אניס ליה, מעלה נסתרות ומפענח נעלמות ובוקע נתיב אורה בהלכות העמומות" (הרב אברהם דובער שפירא מקוונא, **ספר זכרון הרב: קובץ חידושי תורה לזכר... רבי יוסף דוב הלוי סולוביצ׳יק**, בעריכת הרב חיים ירמיהו ווידער ואברהם ירוחם שמידמן, ישיבת רבנו יצחק אלחנן, 1994, בהקדמת הספר.)

having been a youthful prodigy and a distinguished philosophy student, in a way that allows his radiant persona to shine forth; he focuses on the fact that diverse resources converge to emphasize the Rov's preeminence in knowledge and understanding of Torah.

In emphasizing his son's fame, Rav Moshe Soloveitchik wrote: "[As evident by reports in the newspapers in Eretz Yisrael] his Torah and wisdom have preceded him, and many have taken note [of his talents]," and he highlighted the fact that his son is really sui generis: "[Appreciating him] requires a developed insight to comprehend; he brings glory to the Jewish people." He then goes on to cite the Rov's unique achievements:

> In previous generations many imagined that Torah and other branches of wisdom cannot be integrated; however, in this generation we now find Torah and wisdom fully connected. It is found in a person who is a *gedol hador,* an astonishingly great Torah scholar of the generation, equal to the great scholars of previous generations. In addition, his mastery of general wisdom is so great as to make him completely unique in those fields, and he is without a doubt the outstanding Torah scholar of our generation. His understanding [of Torah] carries enormous weight, and his opinion is decisive in all the laws of the Torah, be they simple or complex.

In a subsequent paragraph he refers explicitly to his son's general education and distinguished achievement in philosophy:

> He was a prodigy in his youth, and now the entire Torah is inscribed in his heart...his proficiency is not limited to one area; he has acquired in significant measure also ancillary areas of wisdom which adorn him, and which impart to him grace and splendor. He has attained a doctorate in philosophy with honors from Berlin University, where the professors were astonished by his outstanding talents and with the breadth and depth of his understanding, which they had never before seen. His philosophic originality designates him as a genius of this generation.

The conclusion is powerful and succinct:

> He is a personage who possesses everything: he is a towering figure in his knowledge of Torah, a sovereign genius in the other fields of wisdom, and one of the most talented individuals of the Jewish people today.[15]

4.

This uniqueness also underlies the abundance, the bountifulness, what almost seems to be the ubiquitousness of the Rov's teaching – a

15. [כפי שראיתי בעיתוני א״י] תורתו וחכמתו הלכה לפניו והכריזה עליו... הוא מין בפ״ע [=בפני עצמו] שצריך התכוננות מיוחדה, תכשיט לעם הישראלי... בדורות הקודמים דימו שאי אפשר במציאות להיות תורה ושארי חכמות משולבים יחד. אמנם בדור זה כבר פוגשים תורה וחכמה מחוברים. אבל באופן הזה גדול הדור בתורה באופן מבהיל, כאחד מגדולי הדור בדורות הקודמים, ואם בשארי חכמות באופן גדול הנו היחיד ומיוחד, אין ספק, כי הוא כעת יחיד הדור בהבנת התורה. הבנתו היא משקולת ודעתו היא המכרעת בכל דיני התורה, קלות וחמורות...

היה עילוי וגאון בילדותו ועתה כבר כל התורה חקוקה על לבו... והלא אינו בעל מלאכה אחת. רכש במידה מרובה גם הפרפראות לחכמה, המעטירים אותו, ונותנים לו לוית חן ויופי. השיג את תאר ד״ר פילוסופי׳ באפן הכי מצוין בהאוניברסיטה דברלין, והפרופסורים דשם היו בהתפעלות מגודל כשרונותיו ורוחב הבנתו העמוקה שלא ראו כזאת. ומחדש גם בחכמה זו כגאון הדור...

ואך הוא הגברא דכוליה ביה, גדול התורה בתורה, אב וגאון בשארי חכמות, אחד המיוחדים בכשרונות בין עם ישראל.

(הרב משה סולוביצ׳יק, ״אב מעיד על בנו״, מכתב מיום י״ט באלול תרצ״ה, בתוך **ספר היובל להגרי״ד סולוביצ׳יק**, בעריכת הרב שאול ישראלי ואחרים, [מוסד הרב קוק, תשמ״ד], בסוף כרך א).

Allow me to recreate the following experience. The Kovner Rov, R. Avraham Shapiro, is known for his classic three-volume collection of responsa דבר אברהם. I remember my excitement when I received a posthumously published copy of a volume of דבר אברהם subtitled **חלק הדרוש** (New York, 1949). On page 115, the following note caught my attention:

> ראוי להתעורר על חסרון גדול, שמן ספר העקרים להר״י אלבו ז״ל, לא נתחבר כמעט שום ספר כמתכונתו העוסק באופן שיטתי והתעמקות בעניני הדת ועיקריה, **בהשתמשות עם הספרים והידיעות הנחוצות**, כמו שעשו הראשונים ז״ל, בעוד **שהשעה צריכה מאד** לכך... אמנם ידעתי כי לא מלאכה קלה היא ואין לנו אנשים רבים מוכשרים ומומחים לזה ע״פ חינוכם והכשרתם...

As I read these insightful words, I immediately assumed that he was thinking of the Rov.

fulfillment and manifestation of *ulehorot natan belibo*, "He has put in his heart that he may teach" – the extraordinary ability to communicate ideas and insights is a special gift, a special dimension of genius, for not every person, even one possessed of great learning, is blessed with *ulehorot natan belibo*.[16] The Rov had it and his inspired, disciplined teaching was like a spring flowing with undiminished, ever-increasing strength.

This extraordinary ability was felicitously coupled with his unfailing readiness to teach. I am inclined to suggest that his real greatness lay not in the majesty of his erudition, the force of his originality, or the brilliance of his intuition. (People always admired the sheer pageantry of his learning and were enchanted by the elegance of its various manifestations and formulations.) His greatness – intellectual and moral – lay in his extraordinary ability and amazing readiness to teach and converse effectively, vigorously, and intelligibly on *all* levels; moreover, he did so sympathetically and graciously in a way that simultaneously satisfied and stimulated the listener. In order for the Rov to give a *shiur*, a *derashah*, or a lecture, he had to engage in an act of *tzimtzum*, contraction; he had to restrict and restrain a mighty intellect and channel it, to select prudently from an awesome erudition and a vast reservoir of original insights in a carefully controlled way. The profundities of his learning and the subtleties of his thinking had to be unfolded slowly and methodically. Otherwise, students and listeners would have been overwhelmed, would have drowned in the sea of his Torah. His teaching would not have been intelligible – it would rather become a source of frustration and restlessness. He knew that teaching, no matter how profound, must be pleasant and palatable.

> "Honey and milk are under your tongue." Whoever publicly expounds the words of Torah, and they are not pleasing to their hearers like honey and milk mixed together, it would have been better had he not spoken.[17]

---

16. וּלְהוֹרֹת נָתַן בְּלִבּוֹ (שמות לה, לד). עיינו פירוש ראב"ע על הפסוק – "כי יש חכם גם חרש לא יוכל להורות היטב".

17. דְּבַשׁ וְחָלָב תַּחַת לְשׁוֹנֵךְ. כל מי שאומר דברי תורה ברבים ואינם ערבים על שומעיהם כדבש וחלב המעורבים זה בזה, נוח לו שלא אמרן (**שיר השירים רבה** ד, יא).

Every *shiur*, every speech, was crafted with consummate artistry. This is not only an expression of his literary-conceptual perfectionism but of his realization that if he was to teach effectively, he had to contain his immense learning and unbounded creativity. Style and exposition required sustained attention; hasty writing, like shabby thinking, was intolerable.[18] He had to find the best way to combine felicitous generalization and lucid, compelling interpretation of detail, while interjecting a sprightly parenthetical remark, an anecdotal reference, or a lyrical note. Otherwise we would not have been able to learn from him. He therefore happily fused apparently limitless erudition with enthralling elegance and immense pedagogic skills. When he repeated an idea or interpretation – and the repetition was always eloquent – his intention must have been to guarantee that the presentation was properly textured and fully nuanced, that one theme had been adequately developed and the transition to the next one was crystal clear. Ever mindful of his audience and the goals of his presentation, he used as much learning – *lomdus*, Midrash, philosophy, history, literature – as was necessary and no more.

When I think of him and see him before my eyes preparing and delivering a *shiur*, I am reminded of the following: The Gemara says, in referring to the fact that Hillel had eighty disciples, that "the greatest of them was Yonatan ben Uzziel and the smallest was Rabban Yoḥanan ben Zakkai." The text then continues to depict graphically the greatness of the smallest, least distinguished disciple: he is described as knowing everything.

> They said of Rabban Yoḥanan ben Zakkai that he did not leave [unstudied] Scripture, Mishnah, Gemara, Halakhot, Aggadot, details of the Torah, details of the Scribes, inferences *a minori ad*

18. Long before the famous epigram that the style is the man was formulated, the Talmud underscored the importance of style: "סגנון אחד עולה לכמה נביאים ואין שני נביאים מתנבאים בסגנון אחד" (סנהדרין פט, ב). Rambam emphasized (in *Moreh Nevukhim*, 2:29): "ודע כי לכל נביא, דבר אחד מיוחד בו, כאילו הוא לשון האיש ההוא". Marcel Proust might have cited these references when he said: "Style is in no way a decoration, as some people believe; it is not even a matter of technique; it is – as color is with painters – a quality of vision" (see Peter Gay, *Style in History* [New York, 1974], 5, n. 1). The Rov's style is, as all acknowledge, quite unique.

> *majus*...great matters and small matters. "Great matters" mean the *ma'aseh merkavah*, "small matters" the discussions of Abbaye and Rava.

The stage is set for the Gemara to ask a crucial question: "If the smallest of them was so great, how much more so the greatest?"

However, we are eager to know what remains to be said in laudatory characterization of the greatest; what is the extra dimension that may be identified and attributed to the most distinguished of the disciples? This is the answer: "They said of Yonatan ben Uzziel that when he used to sit and occupy himself with the study of Torah, every bird that flew overhead was immediately burnt."[19]

In studying this remarkable passage and pondering its significance, the yeshiva student focuses on a legal issue to be decided in accord with the *Ḥoshen Mishpat* or *Hilkhot Ḥovel Umazik*: Who has to pay? Who is liable for the damage and the loss? The Kotzker *ḥasid*, conscious of and questing for ecstasy, marvels: If this is how the student is portrayed and celebrated, what is left to describe the teacher? *Vos iz shoin baym rebin?* What unusual resourcefulness does he possess?

To paraphrase the talmudic sentence: If this is what happens with the student, how much more so with the teacher! We seem to have exhausted everything; every factual assessment, every metaphor, every category of praise has been used. Our armamentarium is depleted. The answer of Kotzk was: *Baym rebin vert nisht farbrent*, "Nothing is ever burnt by the rebbe." The master has sovereign control over his mighty resources and uses them with laserlike precision. He creatively summons forth from his reservoir of knowledge and skills only that which is necessary for the task at hand. While revealing one thing, he conceals many things. Nothing is squandered; no available resources are used needlessly or mindlessly. There is no exhibitionism, no ostentatious

---

19. אמרו עליו על רבן יוחנן בן זכאי, שלא הניח מקרא, ומשנה, גמרא, הלכות ואגדות, דקדוקי תורה ודקדוקי סופרים, קלים וחמורים... דבר גדול, ודבר קטן; דבר גדול מעשה מרכבה, דבר קטן הויות דאביי ורבא. וכי מאחר שקטן שבכולם כך, גדול שבכולן על אחת כמה וכמה? אמרו עליו על יונתן בן עוזיאל, בשעה שיושב ועוסק בתורה – כל עוף שפורח עליו מיד נשרף (סוכה כח, א), ועיינו תוספות שם. השוו רמח"ל, **דרך השם**, חלק ד סוף פרק ב.

parade of erudition, no ornamental accumulation of source references. The rebbe produces much light and just enough heat – nothing is burnt and the Torah teaching shines luminously.

The Rov always dispensed his Torah learning in a measured way. He shared his learning graciously and benignly in order to make it possible for others to be partners or participants in the intellectual process. His thorough, meticulous preparation as well as masterful, deliberate presentation were expressions of this. He always prepared very carefully, regardless of the level of his presentation. I recall vividly how he would write out his remarks for the boys and girls of Maimonides School when he came to address them on *Erev Yom Hakippurim* – remarks about the beauty and sanctity of *Yom Hakippurim,* about *taharah,* about the role of the *Kohen Gadol,* about the exaltedness of prayer, about *teshuvah* and *kapparah,* atonement, about the inseparability of mitzvot between man and man and those between man and God, about the striving for moral perfection, about the multiple meanings of *lifnei Hashem,* before God. Everything was carefully crafted even, or especially, for young boys and girls who needed to be reassured and aroused in the quest for understanding and insight, piety and spirituality.

The great master-teacher is described as follows:

> And more than being wise, Kohelet further taught knowledge to the people, and weighed and searched out and framed many maxims.[20]

His learning enables him to teach and disseminate knowledge among the people, among all the people; for this purpose of effective, inspiring teaching, he devises multiple techniques of clarification and exposition and various strategies of explanation. The wise man pays a price for his teaching, which is *torat ḥesed.*[21] For a sage to transmit knowledge and

---

20. וְיֹתֵר שֶׁהָיָה קֹהֶלֶת חָכָם עוֹד לִמַּד דַּעַת אֶת הָעָם וְאִזֵּן וְחִקֵּר תִּקֵּן מְשָׁלִים הַרְבֵּה. (קהלת יב, ט)
21. See Sukkah 49b. Cf. Ḥatam Sofer, *Teshuvot, Yoreh De'ah,* introduction ("פתוחי חותם"). [See *Torah of the Mind and Torah of the Heart,* pp. 19–21.] Actually, the *ḥakham hamasorah,* whose grasp of the tradition is total, is obligated to relate to the totality of the *masorah* community. Everyone has a share in the *masorah,* and therefore none should be excluded from the process of transmission and enhancement which we

have been discussing, no one should be denied the opportunity to benefit from inspired, inspiring teaching. Already the Rambam in his introduction underscored the fact that his monumental codification, the *Mishneh Torah* – a distillation of the entire corpus of Torah literature, broadly conceived – was intended to provide a creative systematization of the Torah and make its contents known to all: **עד שתהא** כולה סדורה **בפי הכל**. With greater emphasis he added: **לקטן ולגדול**.

Everybody will find meaning and insight, guidance and edification. A halakhic formulation that will seem simple and straightforward to an unscholarly or insensitive reader will appear original, provocative, and multifaceted to a scholarly and sensitive reader. "ואפשר שידעם הכל **קטן וגדול**, איש ואישה, בעל לב רחב ובעל לב קצר" (**משנה תורה** הלכות יסודי התורה ד, יג).

The *hakham hamasorah* uses his knowledge and pedagogic skill to write and teach in such a way that two distinct voices may be heard therein, for the small and for the great. He has to achieve the right fusion of popular and sophisticated components, exoteric and esoteric elements. Indeed, the Rambam succeeded in this regard; he remains a teacher of great and small. The echoes and reverberations of the Rambam's great work were heard in different ways by varied members of the community through the ages. It is noteworthy that even the *Moreh Nevukhim* was conceived in such a way that it had something even for beginners. In the introduction, the Rambam states: "I know that among men generally *every beginner* will derive benefit from some of the chapters of this treatise, though he lacks even an inkling of what is involved in speculation. A perfect man, on the other hand, devoted to Law and, as I have mentioned, perplexed, will benefit from all its chapters."

R. Yosef Karo also affirms that his *Shulhan Arukh* was intended to serve beginning students as well as advanced scholars, to increase Torah knowledge among the small and the great. "ומובטח אני בחסד עליון כי על ידי ספר זה תמלא הארץ דעה את ה', הקטנים עם הגדולים, תלמיד עם מבין, חכם חרשים ונבון לחש".

The model for this teaching and transmission is none other than the Almighty, "who teaches Torah to His people Israel." On the verse יַעֲרֹף כַּמָּטָר לִקְחִי תִּזַּל כַּטַּל אִמְרָתִי (דברים לב, ב), R. Ovadiah Sforno comments:

> יַעֲרֹף כַּמָּטָר לִקְחִי: הנה תורתי היא תערוף ותבא בשטף כמטר למבינים המוכנים לקבל מבוע מקור חכמה. תִּזַּל כַּטַּל אִמְרָתִי, ונותנת ג"כ כפי הנגלה כמנה איזו ידיעה להדיוטות שעם היותה מועטת היא טובה מאד כטל, באופן שהיא כִּשְׂעִירִם עֲלֵי דֶשֶׁא, שהמשכילים יביטו נפלאות ממנה, וְכִרְבִיבִים עֲלֵי עֵשֶׂב, שגם ההדיוטות יקנו בה איזה מדע להכיר בו בוראם באופן מה.

The great teacher is walking in the ways of God, fulfilling the mandate of *imitatio dei*, when he takes pains to make his teaching accessible to great and small. Religious-moral imperatives and didactic-pedagogic purposes merge.

We may add, furthermore, that the great teacher knows that his own knowledge and insight are ultimately refined and enhanced by the ability to address "small and

wisdom to the people, not to a pre-selected elite, is to be deflected from his own study and writing, his attainments and advance. Nevertheless, he persists and teaches in a stimulating way. This was the Rov: the rabbi's scholar, the layman's rebbe, the child's guide – all luminous facets of his untiring teaching – *ulehorot natan belibo*.

5.

This remarkable achievement was the consummate expression of combined intellectual and moral prowess – of magnanimity, generosity, and graciousness. The statement in Nedarim comes to mind:

> The Torah was given only to Moshe and his descendants.... Moshe treated it with generosity and gave it to the Jewish people. And about him, the verse says: "He that has a bountiful eye shall be blessed."[22]

The Rov had a very bountiful eye; he was a great *tov ayin*. He shared his wisdom and learning with everyone – rabbis and students, various groups of *ba'alei batim*, young and old, large gatherings and small assemblies. Whether he was interpreting a difficult passage in Tosafot, explicating a particularly recalcitrant formulation by the Rambam, interpreting

---

great" (קטן וגדול), for the reactions of each contribute to full understanding, mature formulation, and judicious interpretation. As the Rambam summed it up:

> וכשם שעץ קטן מדליק את הגדול כך תלמיד קטן מחדד הרב עד שיוציא ממנו בשאלותיו חכמה מפוארה (**משנה תורה** הלכות תלמוד תורה ה, יג).

Let us note the Rov's explicit awareness of this moral-pedagogic feature:

> איש ההלכה הוא פדגוג נפלא, בעל הסברה מצוינת, מזדקק לקטנים ולגדולים ("מה דודך מדוד" [למעלה הערה 11], עמ' 85).

He himself performed this act of *imitatio dei* with zeal and dedication so that heterogeneous audiences were enthralled by his teaching.

See also R. Soloveitchik, *And from There You Shall Seek* (p. 25, n. 30), 147. Note Pesaḥim 109a and Kiddushin 30a.

22. לא ניתנה תורה אלא למשה ולזרעו... משה נהג בה טובת עין ונתנה לישראל ועליו הכתוב אמר: טוֹב עַיִן הוּא יְבֹרָךְ כִּי נָתַן מִלַּחְמוֹ לַדָּל (משלי כב, ט; נדרים לח, א).

a comment of Rashi or Ramban on the Torah, he was always the master teacher – happily and skillfully making his rich learning available to all.

In addition, he felt – and compellingly expressed the idea – that wisdom, like prophecy, was not to be seen as the private possession of an individual. "Neither prophecy nor wisdom is the property of the individual; they belong to everyone."[23] The halakhah obligating a prophet to communicate his prophecy – "a prophet…who suppresses his prophecy…is liable to death at the hands of Heaven"[24] – should govern the behavior and attitude of the wise man, even if a high price is paid. *Noblesse oblige*; the sage is driven to share his learning. The Rov illustrated untiringly the lesson implicit in the opening halakhot of the Rambam, *Hilkhot Talmud Torah*,[25] that studying and teaching constitute one unified mitzvah, one fully integrated performance. As we shall subsequently note, his magnanimity – making his great mind and soul available to those who thirsted for "the word of God" – together with the charm and cogency, pedagogic refinement and rhetorical force of his teaching, resulted in an extraordinarily widespread impact which literally made him *Rabban shel Yisrael.*

6.

These comments on magnanimity and bountifulness lead to one more comment on the Rov's personality. This great man, whose unique scholarship was admired far and wide and whose wise counsel was sought throughout the world, was totally unpretentious, free of all pompousness and officiousness. He deserved and received the greatest respect but never wanted this to be tinged with artificiality. He opened the door, answered the telephone, and conducted all his correspondence without secretaries, without an office staff, without any bureaucracy. His resistance to and antipathy toward mechanization, institutionalization, stodginess, perfunctoriness – above all, artificiality

23. *And from There You Shall Seek* 146. In the original Hebrew:
אין הנבואה, וגם החכמה, קניין היחיד; שייכות הנה לכול, "ובקשתם משם", **איש ההלכה גלוי ונסתר** (ההסתדרות הציונית העולמית, תשל"ט), עמ' 232.

24. נביא... הכובש את נבואתו... מיתתו בידי שמים. (סנהדרין פט, א)

25. *Mishneh Torah, Hilkhot Talmud Torah* 1:1–7, and see *Sefer Hamitzvot,* positive mitzvah 11.

and pretense – carried over to his personal behavior. Just as he was far from being banal and platitudinous in thought or style, so he had no use for the artificial, which is also superficial, in behavior and human relations. The Rov's greatness was thus expressed also in his individuality, personal authenticity, and naturalness in everything he did.

7.

As for his method of Torah teaching – the celebrated Brisker mode of analysis, interpretation and exposition – let me, in the interests of brevity, mention two salient components.

The first component in his method of teaching is that it necessitates treating the Rambam's *Mishneh Torah* not only as a code of Halakhah (as the influential precursor of the *Shulḥan Arukh*), but as a commentary on the Talmud; it recognizes that the Rambam, the authoritative codifier, is *eo ipso* a versatile, original commentator. This premise yields great exegetical-interpretive freedom in reconstructing the implicit commentary. The characterization of a statement as a "difficult Rambam" usually presumes a conventional explanation of the Talmud text or a common form of reconciliation of several texts;[26] when this conventional interpretation fails to illumine the Maimonidean formulation, we are left with a "difficult Rambam." It is self-evident that a curt, normative formulation, a *halakhah pesukah,* in the *Mishneh Torah,* reflects the Rambam's latent explanation of talmudic texts and halakhic concepts – an explanation that often differs from the standard commentators. Consequently, a major task of the rabbinic scholar is to unfold or reconstruct the Rambam's unarticulated interpretive processes; in other words, to compose, by means of fastidious reasoning and disciplined hypothesis, the kind of commentary that the Rambam would have written on the Talmud.

The testimony of R. Menaḥem Hameiri concerning the mode of study followed in his school is particularly informative and enlightening. Having completed the study of a talmudic passage and arrived at what seemed to be the "true explanation" of the passage, he would consult the *Mishneh Torah* in order to find the practical codificatory summation.

26. See Netziv, introduction to his commentary on the *She'iltot.*

Frequently the latter, in its Maimonidean formulation, convinced him that his explanation of the passage was defective or imprecise. The attempt to align the *pesak* with the *sugyah* necessitates intensive intellectual exertion and relies on great ingenuity and resourcefulness. Failure to do this will often leave one with an inadequate understanding.

> I will formulate a rule for you, and I beg your indulgence not to disparage it. Anyone who ignores the final legal ruling [based on the talmudic discussion] will often not comprehend the correct interpretation [of the Talmud] nor will he exert effort to seek it out. By God, many a time it happened that I was sure that I had arrived at a correct interpretation of a halakhic discussion. But upon searching for the correct final ruling in the works of previous authorities, and particularly in the works of the Rav [i.e., Rambam], of blessed memory, which always served me as a final step and the authoritative ruling vis-à-vis other codes of law, I would realize that I did not interpret the halakhic discussion properly.[27]

It is especially interesting, in light of this, to read the Rov's description of how his father was accustomed to study.

> My father always spoke about the Rambam. This is how he would proceed: He would open a volume of the Talmud and read a passage. Then he would say, "This is the interpretation of R. Isaac and the [other] Tosafists; now let us see how the Rambam interpreted the passage." Father would always find that the

27. וכלל אומר לך ומחסדך אל תבוז אליו, והוא שכל מי שלא יחוש לידיעת פסק הענין לא יעלה בידו בהרבה מקומות אמתת הפירוש וגם הוא לא יתעמל בזה. וחי השם, הרבה פעמים קרה על סוגית ההלכה והייתי חושב שכִּוַנתי בה לביאור אמתי, וכשהייתי מחפש לידיעת הפסק בספרי המחברים הקדמונים בפסקיהם ויותר בספרי הרב ז"ל אשר היו לי מכוש אחרון וסוף הוראה לכל החבורים המחברים דרך פסק הייתי מרגיש בעצמי שלא היה ביאור הסוגיא עולה בידי כהוגן (ר' מנחם המאירי, **בית הבחירה** על מסכת ברכות, מהדורת שמואל דיקמן, מכון התלמוד הישראלי השלם, תש"ך, פתיחה לחיבורו, עמ' כח).

> Rambam had offered a different interpretation and had deviated from the simple way.[28]

Hence the biggest challenge and the delightful opportunity provided by the Rambam is the invitation to a disciplined yet imaginative interpretive hypothesis, to a hermeneutic which fuses textual precision with conceptual insight.

I emphasize "disciplined yet imaginative" because that is the key to understanding what is colloquially referred to as a *ḥiddush,* a new interpretation.

8.

A *ḥiddush* is not something contrived or extraneous or completely autonomous, but an age-old, timeless truth waiting to be brought to the surface. It is an inspiring, edifying insight not hitherto perceived, a novel interpretation based upon previously unnoticed associations or connotations, an elegant clarification which resolves hard-core difficulties. A *ḥiddush* is present in Torah, but temporarily invisible. The resourceful, erudite interpreter, using penetrating logic and creative powers of association and differentiation, brings this new-old truth to everyone's attention. This is really what the Ramban is telling us in the introduction to his *Milḥamot Hashem*: "We are obligated to carefully study Torah and mitzvot and to uncover concealed meanings."[29] The highest praise in Brisk was to react to an idea or insight, to a beautiful compelling *ḥiddush,* with the rhapsodic exclamation: *Amitah shel Torah,* "This is the true meaning of Torah!" – i.e., the *ḥiddush* reveals the truth which has not previously been grasped. In the letter which we have already mentioned, the

---

28. *And from There You Shall Seek* (p. 25, n. 30), 143. In the original Hebrew:
אבא מרי דיבר תמיד על אודות הרמב"ם, וכך היה עושה: היה פותח את הגמרא; קורא את הסוגיא. אחר כך היה אומר כדברים האלה: זהו פירושו של הר"י ובעלי־התוספות; עכשיו נעיין נא ברמב"ם ונראה איך פירש הוא. תמיד היה אבא מוצא כי הרמב"ם לא פירש כמותם ומטה מן הדרך הפשוטה. ("ובקשתם משם" [למעלה הערה 23], עמ' 230).

29. החיוב המוטל עלינו לחפש בעניני התורה והמצוות ולהוציא לאור תעלומות מצפונים (רמב"ן, **מלחמות ה'**, הקדמה).

Rov's father says of him: "He is unique in this generation in revealing the *ḥiddush* which expresses the true meaning of Torah."[30]

It is well known that the Talmud in Sukkah characterizes R. Eliezer as never having transmitted a teaching which he did not hear from his teachers; indeed, he himself proclaimed, "I never said anything that I did not hear from my teacher."[31] Yet elsewhere (in *Avot Derabbi Natan*), our Rabbis emphasize that he was the master of doctrines which nobody ever heard prior to his teaching them.[32] Many have correctly suggested that these two descriptions are not contradictory. R. Eliezer's grasp of the *masorah* was so comprehensive, his knowledge so fastidious, his understanding so profound, his intuition so keen, that his *shmu'a*, his tradition, included themes and motifs, premises, conclusions, and insights unknown to others. He elaborated them and they, in turn, became components of the *masorah*.

There are in the Rambam's *Mishneh Torah* hundreds and hundreds of *ḥiddushim* – in addition to those explicitly signaled by the phrase *yera'eh li,* "it seems to me"– which the commentators acknowledge by noting that they are original Maimonidean formulations: "The words of Rabbeinu are appropriate to him"; "It is his own insight, and they are words worthy of being said," and similar phrases. They do not strain to find an explicit source; rather they highlight the novelty, are stimulated by its profundity, savor the felicity of style, power of compression, wealth of allusions, while they experience time and again the delicacy and dynamism of the innumerable original explanations and conclusions. In a word, they confront, admire, and are stimulated by the multisplendored originality.

The *masorah* is deepened and expanded by a great *ḥakham hamasorah* who succeeds in discovering inherent, authentic ideas which have not received any attention or have not been given the primacy and prominence which they deserve and, concomitantly, the opportunity to influence our thinking and behavior.

---

30. הוא יחיד הדור בחידוש התורה לאמיתה. (**ספר היובל להגרי"ד סולוביצ'יק**, למעלה הערה 15)
31. לא אמרתי דבר שלא שמעתי מפי רבי לעולם. (סוכה כח, א)
32. שלא שמעתן אזן מעולם. (**אבות דרבי נתן** נוסחא א, פרק ו)

The Rov, at the beginning of his essay *Ra'ayonot al Hatefillah,* had occasion to comment on this phenomenon, this process of *ḥiddush* (intuitive, authentic interpretation and expansion) as follows:

> All are in need of redemption and liberation: the historical community as well as the individual.... Sometimes an idea remains abandoned and anonymous within systems of thought, until its redeemer who is intimately familiar with it wrests it from isolation and abandonment to freedom and preeminence....
>
> There is redemption within halakhic thought as well. There are [halakhic] postulates that have been relegated to the margins for shorter or longer periods and have strived for deliverance for generations until their liberator arrived and redeemed them. The redeemer is one of the scholars of Israel whom Divine Providence has chosen to extract the approach or the reasoning from its isolation, and to set it at the center of halakhic thought.[33]

It is self-evident that not everyone is qualified or licensed to submit novellae, and not every *ḥiddush* will be absorbed into the mainstream of our *masorah*. When we read the talmudic statement that "anything that a distinguished student (*talmid vatik*) will innovate was included in the original revelation of Torah,"[34] the adjective *vatik* resonates in a special way: only a trusted, thoughtful transmitter, one who carries the *masorah* and contributes to it with dedication, authenticity, and creative understanding, joins the august company of *ḥakhmei hamasorah.* Originality and innovativeness are outgrowths of being saturated with traditional

---

33. הכול זקוקים לגאולה ולפדיון: גם הציבור ההיסטורי, גם היחיד...
לפעמים נשארת אידיאה גלמודה ואלמונית במערכות המחשבה, עד שבא גואלה הקרוב לה ומוציא אותה מבדידותה ומשוממותה לחרות ומעמידה במרכז ...
ישנה גאולה גם במחשבה ההלכתית. ישנן סברות שנידונו לגלות לזמן רב או מועט, וחתרו לגאולה במשך דורות, עד שבא הגואל וגאלם. הגואל הוא אחד מחכמי ישראל שאותו בחרה ההשגחה להוציא את השיטה או הסברה מבדידותה ולהעמידה במרכז המחשבה ההלכתית (הרב יוסף דב סולוביצ'יק, "רעיונות על התפילה", **איש ההלכה גלוי ונסתר** [למעלה הערה 23], עמ' 239).

34. ואפילו מה שתלמיד וותיק עתיד להורות [גרסת הגר"א "לחדש"] לפני רבו כבר נאמר למשה מסיני (ירושלמי, פאה ב, ד).

categories and concepts. There is a weighty inducement to novelty but it is accompanied by a deep sense of responsibility and accountability.

9.

It should be noted that mighty historical challenges – conditions of adversity, tendencies to decline, symptoms of erosion – elicit especially creative responses from these great sages who are the guardians and interpreters of the *masorah.* My son Reb Mayer called attention to the complementary terminology used by the Rambam to describe the *ḥakhmei hamasorah:* they are *ma'atikei hashmu'ah* and *magideha,*[35] transmitters of tradition and its interpreters. Actually, the Rov commented on the significance of the phrase *mak'ḥish magideha* in *Hilkhot Teshuvah* 3:8, in his famous *shiur* on *kiddush haḥodesh.*[36] *Ḥakhmei hamasorah* counter the challenges, which ordinarily produce pessimism and demoralization, with intellectual creativity and spiritual virtuosity, which can only result in optimism and revitalization. These wise men, teachers par excellence, inexhaustible sources of inspiration and commitment, sustain and advance the authoritative *masorah.*[37]

10.

The second component[38] in his method of teaching is that the primary mode of interpretation used in this process is abstract conceptualization, i.e., to find or extrapolate the unarticulated idea, the unperceived association, the unifying or differentiating characteristic which informs the plethora of details, to identify and analyze the concept which undergirds the many apparently disparate facts. This often involved the imaginative translation of facts into ideas; "pots and pans" become abstract concepts. The method probes into the inner strata of talmudic logic and formulates the disparities as well as similarities between various passages in the light of conceptual analysis. Complex concepts, discussed

35. **מעתיקי השמועה** (**משנה תורה**, הקדמה); מכחיש מגידיה (**משנה תורה** הלכות תשובה ג, ח).

36. הרב משה סולוביצ׳יק ובנו ותלמידו ר׳ יוסף דוב הלוי סולוביצ׳יק, **קובץ חידושי תורה: אסופת מאמרים** (מכון ירושלים, תשמ״ד), עמ׳ סא.

37. See the concluding section of this chapter.

38. See sec. 7 above.

fragmentarily in numerous sections of the Talmud or unrelated contexts of the Maimonidean code, are defined with vigor and precision, with dialectical insight and acuity.

11.

This entire method, which at the risk of oversimplification I have reduced to its most essential features, lends dignity to Torah, enhances *kevod hatorah,* the honor of the Torah. Original and profound, elegant and enthralling, such novel interpretations combining massive erudition with great intuition speak not only to one's religious consciousness but fully engage the mind as well. They powerfully rebut the platitudinous Haskalah indictment of Talmud study as intellectually insipid and spiritually stultifying. There is not only technical proficiency and extensive knowledge but intellectual-aesthetic delight in the process of learning. By his mastery and repercussive application of this method, as a result of readily discernible extraordinary sophistication and generally admired unfailing originality, the Rov enhanced *kevod hatorah.* His teaching was intellectually exciting and religiously uplifting.

There is a story that when the Rov's great-grandfather, the Beit Halevi, met Reb Yisrael Salanter, he would repeat to him some *ḥiddushim* of his son Reb Ḥayyim, the most forceful protagonist, if not the originator, of this approach in modern times. Reb Yisrael Salanter, who was very much attuned to contemporary nineteenth-century developments coming in the wake of emancipation and enlightenment, and who agonized over the negative phenomena which he observed, responded as follows: "The next generation will study Torah that way and we shall overcome the Haskalah." What are we to make of this remarkable statement? What is the connection between the two parts of his statement?

Reb Yisrael Salanter meant to say that in addition to the religious-metaphysical commitment which must be nurtured and sustained, young people need intellectual challenge and intellectual satisfaction. He knew well that many thought, mistakenly, that the Haskalah provided this kind of intellectual excitement; that is why an analytic-conceptual method, equal to any in its rigor and profundity, in its vigorous discipline and its invigorating results, would rehabilitate Halakhah while repudiating the Haskalah.

The Rov does not tell this story, as far as I know, but I found one sentence in his eulogy on his uncle the Brisker Rov which makes the same point very poignantly. In that remarkable, revelatory essay, which contains a spirited characterization of Reb Ḥayyim's method more sharply delineated than what is described in *Ish Hahalakhah,* the Rov asks about his grandfather's decisive impact: "What was the source of [R. Ḥayyim's] power that if not for him, Torah would have been forgotten and *we would have been unable to disseminate it in that period*?"[39]

What was the secret of his genius? If not for his trailblazing, stimulating, widely repercussive achievement, we would not be able to teach and disseminate Torah.

The Rov, who frequently emphasized the importance of enhancing *kevod hatorah,* who saw this as the assignment given us in this age by Divine Providence, was privileged to do this more than anyone else. He was the teacher who disseminated Torah in this age with verve and zeal, emphasizing the nobility of the intellectual process, the exhilaration of learning, the beauty of Torah study.[40] The same statement that he made about his grandfather is applicable to him: "What was the source of his power…?"

We should note that the Rov's early *ḥiddushei Torah* deal with themes of *zera'im,* agriculture, and *kodoshim,* the sacrificial service in the Temple; they are markedly original and completely classical in theme and format. He appropriated Reb Ḥayyim's approach and individualized it by his erudition, clarity of insight, and mode of exposition. His innovations and acuity, using a method characterized by innovation, are salient. Subsequently, he chose to concentrate on themes of prayer, benedictions, Torah reading, festivals, and fast days – these are, of course, the topics of his celebrated *yahrzeit shiurim.* He sought themes that had not been studied in this way. Dichotomies between technical-theoretical and popular-practical were not real; topics considered to be popular, well known, and accessible were transformed by his profoundly original and repercussive analysis.

---

39. במה היה כחו יפה, שאילמלא הוא הייתה משתכחת תורה מישראל **ולא היינו יכולים להרביץ אותה בתקופה זו** ("מה דודך מדוד" [למעלה הע' 11], עמ' 70).

40. עיינו רמח"ל (למעלה הערה 19).

12.

The other major area of his teaching, which is conventionally described as his philosophy, is, in my opinion, best seen – to use traditional religious categories – as his incessant, inspired preoccupation with *penimiyut hatorah* or *nishmat hatorah,* the inner spirituality of Torah. One utilizes contemporary philosophic terminology and phenomenology – which is a stylistic, conceptual requirement basic to the very enterprise – but one's goal is the same as that of the great thinkers of previous generations: to penetrate to the inner core of Torah, to expound its essential beliefs, to explain what is contained in mitzvot, to unfold their teleology (which is sometimes explicit and sometimes allusive), to understand the dynamics of *Torah shebe'al peh* and its axiology, and hence to deepen one's comprehension and to intensify one's experience. This endeavor is not extraneous to Torah, not independent of Halakhah, but is an integral, indispensable part of it. As the Ramban put it, "Study of the Torah's [core] beliefs is itself Torah study."[41] It is not merely an intellectual indulgence or a concession to the attraction of philosophic study, but the fulfillment of a basic religious duty. Use of philosophic language and conceptualization is integral; indeed, it may provide the stimulus for an analysis which yields new insights in the realm of *penimiyut hatorah.*

The Rov illustrated vividly and powerfully the meaning and majesty of the Rambam's formulation in *Hilkhot Teshuvah* concerning the instrumental relationship between wide-ranging philosophic knowledge and the ultimate religious attainment.

> It is a truth clearly known that love for the Holy One, blessed be He, becomes bound up in a person's heart – so that he is always rightly enthralled by it, and forsakes all else, as He charged, "[Love the Lord your God] with all your heart and all your soul" – only through such knowledge as he has of Him. As is the knowledge, so is the love: if [the one be] little, [the other will be] little; if [the one be] great, [the other will be] great. One must, therefore, be single-minded in mastering and reflecting on the

41. לימוד אמונת התורה הוא הלימוד בתורה. (**ספר המצוות לרמב"ם עם השגות הרמב"ן** [למעלה עמ' 31 הערה 45] שכחת הלאוין ב').

disciplines and sciences that give him such knowledge of his Master as humans can fathom and grasp.[42]

This resonant formulation highlights the inexorable link between knowledge of God and love of God; it provides a double spiritualistic teleology for a comprehensive and rigorous intellectualism. Wide-ranging philosophic knowledge leads to knowledge of God, which in turn is a prerequisite for love of God. Indeed, no attempt is made, here or elsewhere, to camouflage or gloss over the robust intellectualism – only to emphasize its true spiritual purpose.

We may say that the Rov disproved the assumption of practically all religious philosophers since William James that "primary experience and conceptual articulation are always at odds with each other," that there is a difference between "philosophy of religion as dialectic of ideas and living religion in its 'pristine form.'"[43] The Rov's point of departure – his method, his objective – was not formal scholastic philosophy of religion, which he knew well in all its guises, but rather a glorious *masorah* of *ahavat Hashem, de'ot,* and *talmud Torah,* of *Zohar* and *Sha'arei Orah,* of *Reishit Ḥokhmah* and *Likkutei Torah*; a *masorah* in which the dialectic of ideas provides a natural, nurturing framework for the primary religious experience and for the open-ended, ongoing religious quest. He is in the tradition of the *Ḥovot Halevavot* (e.g., introduction, book 1, book 5) and of that ever-fascinating chapter 51 of the third part of the *Moreh Nevukhim,* which insisted that profound knowledge of God is necessary for the true service of God. This is intellectualism, to be sure, but not a self-contained or self-sufficient intellectualism. It is intellectualism with a higher purpose which thus bridges what seems to be a yawning chasm between dialectical analysis and philosophical

42. דבר ידוע וברור, שאין אהבת הקדוש ברוך הוא נקשרת בליבו של אדם, עד שישגה בה תמיד כראוי ויעזוב כל שבעולם חוץ ממנה, כמו שציוה ואמר "בכל לבבך ובכל נפשך", אלא בדעה שידעהו. ועל פי הדעה על פי האהבה, אם מעט מעט ואם הרבה הרבה. לפיכך צריך האדם ליחד עצמו להבין ולהשכיל בחכמות ותבונות המודיעין לו את קונו, כפי כח שיש באדם להבין ולהשיג (**משנה תורה** הלכות תשובה י, ו).

43. See the introduction by John E. Smith to his edition of William James, *The Varieties of Religious Experience* (Harvard University Press, 1985).

discourse on one side and subjective experience and normative religious action on the other.

13.

I want to clarify a bit more the role of philosophy. There is, in my opinion, no justification for debate or equivocation concerning the Rov's relation to general culture – philosophy, science, literature – but it is necessary to put this in a proper perspective. The facts are unmistakable. He achieved sovereign mastery of these fields and used his knowledge selectively, creatively, and imaginatively, with great philosophic acumen and originality. He often reminisced with me about his student years and his unquenchable thirst for knowledge, which, he said, was characteristic of many of his contemporaries. He recalled that straitened material circumstances never dampened his enthusiasm for study. The impact of those years on him was great and lasting; his quest for wide-ranging scientific-humanistic knowledge was successful. The record of his dedicated quest for and ongoing use of this knowledge is clear and unambiguous.

The following may be a useful way of approaching this topic. If you knew nothing about the Rambam's programmatic statements concerning the religious value of the process of intellectualization, his ideological conviction concerning the indispensability of philosophy for Torah, his passionate commitment to demonstrating the inseparability and complementarity of two apparently discordant but intrinsically harmonious domains (referred to as *gufei Torah* and *yesodot gufei Torah*);[44] if you were not acquainted with these forcefully articulated positions and merely studied the *Commentary on the Mishnah* – the most popular of his writings – you would be struck by the multiple contexts in which philosophy, philosophers, and philosophic ideas appear. Indeed, you need read only the introduction to the commentary on *Pirkei Avot, Shemonah Perakim,* and the commentary on *Pirkei Avot* itself and you

44. [That is, Halakhah and meta-Halakhah. See Rambam, *Commentary on the Mishnah,* Ḥagigah 2:1.]

will encounter directly his extensive use of philosophy, repeated references to philosophers, and incisive analysis of philosophic problems. There is no need for any *a priori* statement of intention or a methodological-ideological prologue. His actions, his words, the message which he communicates to his readers by the scope, style, and subtlety of his writing tell the entire story. The ready, abundant references and forceful disquisitions buttress his reputation as an enthusiastic propagator of philosophy and a creative religious philosopher.

Similarly, if you knew nothing about the Rov's biography and merely studied the *Ish Hahalakhah* (published in 1944), you would confront a massive, strategic reliance on the history of philosophy and science. The first two pages introduce you to Hegel, Kierkegaard, Rudolph Otto and Karl Barth, Eduard Spranger and Ferdinand Lasalle, Rousseau, Nietzsche, Bergson, Spengler, and Heidegger – a breathtaking list. A page later you meet Plato and Aristotle, Galileo and Newton and soon thereafter Husserl, Scheler, Berkeley, and Hermann Cohen. If you persisted and made your way to the end of this remarkable philosophical-spiritual meditation, the very last note refocuses your attention on a cast of influential figures: Kant and Hermann Cohen, Kierkegaard, Ibsen, Scheler, and Heidegger together with the Rambam and Ibn Gabirol, and then once again, after a passing reference to Duns Scotus, on to Schopenhauer and Nietzsche. These references reflect not only great erudition and precision in the history of philosophy but also a philosophic temper, a philosophic mode of thinking, a subtle, analytical mind.

In addition, we may note certain propositions, affirmations or generalizations which stand out. For example, the following sentence summarizing the views of many thinkers concerning *toda'ah datit*, religious consciousness (perhaps the major motif in the Rov's writings), in the opening paragraph of the *Ish Hahalakhah* is enthralling:

> There is much truth to the fundamental contention set forth both by the dialectical philosophies of Heraclitus and Hegel with regard to the ongoing course of existence in general, and the views of Kierkegaard, Karl Barth, and Rudolph Otto with

> regard to the religious consciousness and its embodiment in the experience of *homo religiosus* in particular, namely, that there is a creative power imbedded within antithesis.[45]

The halakhic master invites the reader to ponder carefully certain philosophical and theological classics which illumine the antithetical structure of religious experience and creativity – the theme which enthralled him.

Similarly, the following sweeping generalization concerning Christian theology in *Kol Dodi Dofek* – the great manifesto of religious Zionism – also arrests your attention by virtue of its authoritativeness and comprehensiveness:

> One must have a comprehensive knowledge of theological literature, from Justin Martyr to contemporary theologians in order to understand the enormous miracle of the public repudiation of a central axiom of Christian theology.[46]

In the evocative eulogy of his uncle, the Brisker Rov, the Rov finds it useful and appropriate to characterize the innovative aspects of Reb Ḥayyim Brisker's method by positioning it in the framework of the conceptualization and mathematization of nature developed by the founders of classical and modern physics from Galileo and Newton until our own time. He then suggests, a bit further in the same essay, that there is a basic analogy between Kant's declaration concerning the independence of pure reason and Reb Ḥayyim's insistence upon the autonomy of the reason of Halakhah:

---

45. R. Soloveitchik, *Halakhic Man* (p. 103, n. 56), p. 142, n. 4.
יש הרבה מן האמת במשנתם הדיאלקטית של הירקליט והגל בנוגע לתהליך ההוויה בכלל, ובהשקפתם של קירקגור, קרל ברט ורודולף אוטו ביחס אל התודעה הדתית והתגלמות הוויתו של איש הדת בפרט, שכוח יוצר נטוע באנטיתזה ("איש ההלכה", **איש ההלכה גלוי ונסתר** [למעלה הערה 23], עמ' 12).

46. יש צורך בידיעה מקיפה בספרות התיאולוגית, מאז ימי יוסטין מרטיר עד התיאולוגים החדשים בימינו, כדי להבין את כל הפלא הגדול הזה, שעל ידו נפרכה בפומבי ההנחה המרכזית בתיאולוגיה הנוצרית ("קול דודי דופק", **דברי הגות והערכה** [למעלה הערה 11], עמ' 25).

> Kant, in his time, proclaimed the autonomy of pure reason of scientific-mathematical cognition. R. Ḥayyim fought the war of independence for halakhic reason and demanded on its behalf total autonomy.[47]

The clarity and naturalness of the comparisons underscore that this mode of reference and of perception (using universal concepts and moving from the general to the particular) is integral to his way of thinking and exposition. That is the way to clarify, to conceptualize, or to put in perspective; that way of conceptualization and exposition provides the infrastructure of all his writing.

Particularly striking in this context are the citations from belles lettres, e.g., Tolstoy's *Death of Ivan Ilitch*, Ibsen, Stefan Zweig's article on Tolstoy (which is introduced for purposes of comparison with Reb Ḥayyim), Y. L. Peretz's *Bonze Shweig*, Heinrich Heine's *Reisebilder*, or the theory of literature (Aristotle's *Poetics)*. I note parenthetically that the Rov liked literature and appreciated good literary criticism; he could easily have been a literary critic – erudite and insightful.

All this is a given – crystal clear, absolutely incontestable, and very meaningful.

14.

What is distinctive is the fact that the Rov does not preach or cajole, persuade or brainwash; he does not present an elaborate rationale for the study of philosophy. The latter simply appears as part of his intellectual capital; he uses it freely and wisely and effectively in his various expositions and explorations of Jewish thought. The Rov's philosophic and homiletical corpus has *no apologetics*; there is no attempt to argue and demonstrate the importance of general learning as an abstract proposition, just as there is no attempt to defend or glorify Western culture. Similarly, there is no attempt to demonstrate that traditional Judaism is completely congruent with philosophy (or any part of it). This truly

47. קאנט בשעתו הכריז על עצמאותה של התבונה הטהורה של ההכרה המדעית־מתמאטית; ר׳ חיים נלחם את מלחמת השחרור של תבונת ההלכה ותבע לה אוטונומיה שלמה (״מה דודך מדוד״ [למעלה הערה 11], עמ׳ 78).

noteworthy feature is a result of the fact that for the Rov there was nothing essentially problematic about the *masorah*; he did not feel compelled to prove that Torah and philosophy or science are compatible. Neither Kant nor Kierkegaard, Hegel nor Husserl are sources of authoritative norms or principles to which Judaism *must* conform. Rather, Kant and Kierkegaard, Bergson and James, and many other figures from classical to contemporary thought provide a reservoir of ideas and insights, concepts and categories to be used critically and constructively in the analysis and clarification of aspects of the *masorah* – indeed, in the attempt to portray and explain the traditional, often-maligned talmudist or to enhance one's appreciation for the unique religious significance of Halakhah. The clichés of the history of Jewish thought – synthesis, symbiosis, harmony, reconciliation – are missing from his vocabulary and are not applicable to his teaching. His all-encompassing philosophic, scientific, and humanistic knowledge served him for his own purposes – for creative, enthralling exposition, for urbane, intelligent discourse, for subtle, sophisticated commentary on Torah ideas.

Indeed, I think that what the Rov reports in the name of Reb Ḥayyim Brisker concerning the proper understanding of the famous midrash on the *akeidah* is emblematic of his intellectual position. The midrash says that only *after* the angel told Avraham not to harm the young Yitzḥak did he inquire of God: "On the one hand You told me yesterday that 'it is through Yitzḥak that offspring shall be continued for you,' and on the other hand now You said to me, 'Take your son, your only son, and offer him as a sacrifice.'"[48] The drama of the *akeidah* is not only in binding Yitzḥak on the altar but also in the inner struggle of Avraham to avoid positing even for a moment that God's words are contradictory: "He did not, Heaven forbid, understand God's words as contradicting themselves."[49]

His faith had to remain consistent and unfragmented. When the angel's appearance resolved the apparent contradiction – the apparent

48. אתמול אמרת לי כִּי בְיִצְחָק יִקָּרֵא לְךָ זָרַע, ועכשיו אמרת לי קַח נָא אֶת בִּנְךָ אֶת יְחִידְךָ ... וְהַעֲלֵהוּ שָׁם לְעֹלָה (ירושלמי תענית ב, ד).

49. שלא תפס את דברי ה׳ כאילו, חס ושלום, הכחישו אהדדי. (״איש ההלכה״ [למעלה הערה 23], עמ׳ 15, הערה 5).

absurdity and self-negation of two such antithetical statements – only then was Avraham free to ask. The Rov quotes his grandfather's interpretation:

> As long as the third, harmonizing, verse had not yet been revealed, Avraham had no right to question God's word, and for this reason he contained himself until the end of the epic.

and then adds his peroration:

> The pangs of consciousness of the man of God and the towering and awesome strength of his self-restraint shine forth here in a clear and pure light.[50]

We recognize the significance and forcefulness of this statement, for descriptions of the religious consciousness – the self-awareness, turbulence, and steadfast commitment of the *homo religiosus* – are among the salient, recurrent themes of the Rov's writing. This formulation reflects a man of perfect faith who does not feel a need to look for external justification or adventitious vindication. Faith, the motive force and defining norm in the behavior and thought of the *homo religiosus,* needs to be understood, to be analyzed and internalized; its demands may be challenging, but its essence is restraint, discipline, and commitment.

The Rov's teaching is not cast as an apology for traditional Judaism or as an attempt to harmonize it with some general school of thought. The *masorah* is not subordinated to any extraneous system, nor does it need to be validated by aligning it with Kant or Hegel. It needs to be appropriated and explicated, to be analyzed and conceptualized. The Rov's teaching – drawing freely from Torah and *ḥokhmah* – fascinates us for its compelling interpretive insights and uncanny intuitions, its theological subtleties, philosophical perceptions, and moral nuances, its

---

50. R. Soloveitchik, *Halakhic Man* (p. 103, n. 56), 143, note 5.
כל זמן שהכתוב השלישי המכריע לא בא, לא היה אברהם רשאי לשאל ולפיכך התאפק עד סוף המחזה... ייסורי התודעה של איש האלקים וכוח הבלגתו הענקי והנורא בוקעים כאן באור בהיר וזך ("איש ההלכה" שם, למעלה הערה 23).

beauty and profundity. We are never told to be defensive or apologetic. The Rov's message is the following: When you know your way – your point of departure and goals – then use philosophy, science, and the humanities to illumine your exposition, sharpen your categories, probe the profundities and subtleties of the *masorah*, and reveal its charm and majesty; in so doing, you should be able to command respect from the alienated, and communicate with some who might otherwise be hostile or indifferent to your teaching, as well as to increase the sensitivity and spirituality of the committed.

The discussion of the *akeidah* is completely congruent with the Rov's finely honed comments on the significance of the cosmological and ontological proofs for the existence of God – an axial theme in the history of philosophy. The Rov emphasizes with great passion that these proofs should *not* be seen as logical, objective, epistemologically valid, but as expressions of man's natural yearning for God. "We do not need these demonstrations as proofs, because the experience of God is the basis of certainty."[51]

Direct religious experience guarantees absolute certitude; logical inferences from the finite to the infinite, from the temporal to the eternal are insignificant and pale in comparison. Proofs should be seen as functions of direct religious experiences, not based on the process of logical deduction, not making scientific-epistemological claims. "The religious sensibility does not offer decisive proofs, draw inferences, or make deductions. It 'senses' and experiences God in its innermost ontological consciousness."[52]

Again we return to the nature of "religious consciousness," which makes the experience of the living God part of the ontological awareness. The religious consciousness is not to be subservient to or derivative from any philosophic impetus; indeed, it is powerful and plays a leadership role in philosophical reflection. This is the thrust of Reb

51. R. Soloveitchik, *And from There You Shall Seek* (p. 25, n. 30), 157, note 3.
אין אנו זקוקים למופתים אלה לשם הוכחה, כי הלא חווית האלקים היא יסוד הוודאיות.
("ובקשתם משם" [למעלה הערה 23], עמ' 127 הערה 3)

52. R. Soloveitchik, *And from There You Shall Seek*, p. 13.
אין התודעה הדתית חותכת מופתים, אין היא מקישה ולא מסיקה, 'מרגישה' היא וחיה את האלוה בתוך תוכה של התודעה האונטולוגית. ("ובקשתם משם", עמ' 129, שם)

Ḥayyim's statement about two passages which contradict one another. This is the upshot of the Rov's statement concerning proofs of the existence of God. The context is different, the vocabulary is different, the religious-intellectual position is the same.

Such a perspective highlights the uniqueness of the Rov's teaching, in comparison to both modern Jewish thinkers and to the *Rishonim* as well. Unlike R. Azriel Hildesheimer, who devoted his immense learning to showing, *inter alia,* that there was no conflict between the philological-historical methods of modern scholarship and traditional views and assumptions; unlike R. Samson Raphael Hirsch or R. Reines or R. Kook who, with varying degrees of success or consistency, elaborated philosophic, meta-historical conceptualizations explaining the importance of Western culture; unlike those nineteenth- and twentieth-century thinkers who believed that Judaism had to be vindicated and verified in terms of contemporary European philosophy, the Rov made no sophisticated arguments on behalf of philosophy and did not engage in intricate apologetics. There is no confrontation with philosophy. Synthesis was not the driving force of his system. He mastered philosophy – it was a valuable part of his intellectual endowment. He then selected from his magisterial erudition what was useful and constructive, insightful and enhancing – e.g., Kant on the noumenon-phenomenon, Bergson on epistemological pluralism, Otto on the nature of the holy, Kierkegaard on the existentialist critique of Hegelianism, Barth on the role of dialectics and antithetical categories – and used ideas strategically and effectively. Of course, he did the same, *mutatis mutandis,* with the *Moreh Nevukhim* and the *Tanya.* His blessed combination of massive knowledge and great originality enabled him to formulate and express axial religious ideas in a universal philosophic language as well as a particularly Jewish idiom – a special kind of *lishna derabban,* a rabbinic parlance.

This is the secret of his extraordinary, creative philosophic writing; he was not artificially constrained by any one school.[53] He did not have

53. He once commented to me that the Ramban may have been conceptually more creative than the Rambam for this very reason. The Rambam was subject to Aristotelian constraints and operated within a clearly defined philosophic framework. The Ramban was unfettered. Note that Julius Guttman (*Philosophies of Judaism* [Holt,

to conform in a rigid, scholastic way to any system. His works reflect the same structural pattern: abstract analytical-dialectical philosophical writing laced with lyrical flashes, autobiographical reminiscences, and touching scenes based on familial lore or related generally to *ḥakhmei hamasorah.* While the philosophic exposition is erudite and enlightening, the impetus and the objective of his writings are distinctly religious; generically they belong to the great religious literature of all times.

Hence, to look for apparent contradictions and inconsistencies in his various works, to quibble whether his premises and arguments are medieval or modern, rationalistic or pietistic, to argue whether his thought should be described as existentialist or dialectical, Kierkegaardian or neo-Kantian, is not very edifying. He was neither Kantian nor Kierkegaardian and he could be both. While he had the intellectual ability and resourcefulness to expound their ideas vigorously and critically, what he chose to do was to use them carefully and selectively for his constructive-expository purposes. The apparent contradictions reflect his dialectical style of writing, his effective use of typologies in which opposite phenomena and antithetical attitudes are elucidated. In addition, it has been frequently noted that style is a mixture of self-expression and self-control, of exposition and concealment; in our idiom we would describe this dialectic as "More than what I have read before you

---

Rinehart and Winston, 1964], 153) said the same thing with regard to the Rambam: "But there is also such a thing as originality of creative synthesis."

I think that something I wrote many years ago about the Ramban is applicable to the Rov: "He had profound all-embracing conceptions of God, Israel, history, and the world, and his total *anschauung* needs to be meticulously reconstructed. He defies facile categorization, as evidenced, for example, by his agile critique of philosophy and deft use of philosophic materials and ideas." See my *Rabbi Moses Naḥmanides (Ramban): Explorations in His Religious and Literary Virtuosity* (Harvard University Press, 1983), 7. It is worth mentioning here that the Rov was drawn to the halakhic analysis found in *Milḥamot Hashem* and *Ḥiddushei Haramban* and frequently pointed out similarities in modes of reasoning between the Ramban and Reb Ḥayyim Brisker. As is known, the Rov contributed significantly to reviving the study of the Ramban's *Peirush al Hatorah;* he certainly agreed with the saying of the Ḥatam Sofer:

ספרי הרמב"ן מצויים אלא שעוסקיו אינם מצויים (**שו"ת חתם סופר** חלק ו', ליקוטים סימן סא).

is written here"[54] or 'The words of Torah can be succinct in their context, but ample in other contexts."[55] Therefore, it is only natural, quite predictable, and fully understandable that the degree of expression and control will vary, that different modes of self will be selectively expressed, that we will find varying exposures, different modalities, and successive moods – all of which, taken together, produce a complete, polychromatic picture. We must avoid fragmentation of his literary corpus, be wary of extrapolating one theme or one segment and analyzing it in isolation. The Archimedean points of his teaching always need to be identified.[56]

15.

The *ḥakhmei hamascrah* who are chosen to affect the destiny of the Jewish people *often* appear at a critical juncture in history – at a time of fatigue and frustration, social despair and intellectual gloom, when Torah study seems to be in irreversible decline and its very continuity threatened as a result of historical vicissitudes and inexorable, apparently insurmountable pressures. I emphasize "often" because obviously there is an unbroken chain of *ḥakhmei hamasorah*, of *ma'atikei hashmu'ah*, those who perpetuate the *masorah* by teaching others; but times of crisis bring forth especially creative sages, driven by a mission and a vision, whose role is crucial and whose influence is profound and reinvigorating. The powerful words of the Rambam, simultaneously frightening and energizing, resonate in our minds:

"In our days," Maimonides states in the introduction to the *Mishneh Torah*, "all feel the pressure of hard times. The wisdom of our wise men has disappeared, the understanding of our prudent men is hidden";[57] this motif from Yeshayahu (29:14), the disappearance of the

---

54. יותר ממה שקריתי לפניכם כתוב כאן. (סוטה מ, ב)

55. דברי תורה עניים במקומן ועשירים במקום אחר. (ירושלמי, ראש השנה ג, ה)

56. וכל המניח הדברים שביארנו שהם בנויים על יסודי עולם והולך ומחפש בהגדה מן ההגדות או במדרש או בדברי אחד הגאונים ז"ל עד שימצא מלה אחת על פשטה, ישיב בה על דברינו שהן דברי דעת ותבונה – אינו אלא מאבד עצמו לדעת... אלא כך ראוי למי שהוא מבין ולבו נכון למול דרך האמת: שישים ענין זה המפורש בתורה עיקר, ויסוד שלא יֵהרס, ויתד התקועה שלא תמיש ("איגרת לר' עובדיה הגר", **איגרות הרמב"ם**, מהדורת ש"לת, עמ' רלו-רלז).

57. ובזמן הזה תכפו צרות יתירות, ודחקה השעה את הכל, ואבדה חכמת חכמינו ובינת נבונינו נסתתרה (**משנה תורה**, הקדמה).

wisdom of our wise men, becomes a standard slogan describing the worrisome decline in scholarship, as evidenced by its use in the introduction to the *Tur* and the *Shulḥan Arukh*. At such a time of intellectual-spiritual eclipse, the Rambam felt that he had to act boldly and heroically: "I, Moses the son of Maimon the Sephardi, bestirred myself… to compose a work from which the entire Oral Law might become systematically known to all… so that all the rules shall be accessible to young and old."[58] His response to a critical situation characterized by diminishing knowledge of Torah was to compose a comprehensive, systematic work that could be studied by great and small, learned and unlearned. This was a novel, daring enterprise – an act of intellectual and religious courage.

It is noteworthy that a similar sense of crisis, of challenge and response, underlies his description of the period of R. Yehudah Hanasi and his momentous redaction of the Mishnah. "And why did our holy master act thus [to reduce the oral tradition to writing] and not leave the matter as it was? Because he saw that the disciples were becoming few, and new troubles were coming upon them."[59]

The chaotic and unsettled conditions of the country, the widespread demographic-social instability, the crushing confrontation with destructive historical forces brought in their wake a serious impoverishment of the people's spiritual-intellectual forces. R. Yehudah Hanasi was stationed on the crest of a great wave of learning, and before his contemporaries and successors fell into the troughs, he had to act decisively. The redaction of the Mishnah, like the *Mishneh Torah* many centuries later, was a novel, daring achievement. R. Yehudah Hanasi and, consciously following him, R. Moshe ben Maimon were *ḥakhmei hamasorah* who acted creatively, courageously, and decisively to safeguard the *masorah*.

Recent sages, fully aware of the nexus between crisis and creativity in the history of our *masorah*, reflected upon the etiology and

58. ומפני זה נערתי חצני, אני משה ברבי מיימון הספרדי... לחבר דברים המתבררים מכל אלו החיבורים... עד שתהא תורה שבעל פה כולה סדורה בפי הכל... עד שיהיו כל הדינים גלויים לקטן ולגדול (שם).

59. ולמה עשה רבינו הקדוש כך... ולא הניח הדבר כמות שהיה? לפי שראה שתלמידים מתמעטים והולכים, והצרות מתחדשות ובאות... (שם). [וראו דברי הרב טברסקי בספרו **כמעיין המתגבר: הלכה ורוח ביצירת חכמי ימי הביניים** בעריכת כרמי הורוביץ (מרכז שזר, תש"ף, עמ' 91 והלאה).]

teleology of this phenomenon. Let us note two beautiful, resonant examples. The illustrious founder of Gerer Ḥasidism, known as the Ḥiddushei Harim – a spiritual-intellectual giant of formidable resources who guided Polish Jewry during the first half of the nineteenth century and whose influence remains widespread – provides insight into this phenomenon by commenting on R. Akiva and his troubled, turbulent, traumatic times. The terse comment of the Ḥiddushei Harim contains an entire philosophy of Jewish history, a religious conceptualization of the development of Torah study focusing especially on why there are periods of strikingly intense creativity and overwhelming originality.

> This is what *Ḥazal* meant when they cite the verse in Iyov, "And all precious things his eye has seen," and explain, "Matters not revealed to Moshe were revealed to R. Akiva and his friends." For R. Akiva lived at the time of the destruction (of the Temple) and it was necessary to cause the light of the Torah to shine with greater intensity. How much more so is it necessary [that commentaries to the Torah must light our way to ensure our continued existence] in later generations, for we have lost all because of our sins, and all that remains is the Torah, as it is written, "Had not Your teachings been my delight, I would have perished in my affliction." … For that reason there are times in these generations that the words of Torah shine with greater depth, with the hope that with their merit, our hearts will turn to God, blessed be He.[60]

Because R. Akiva lived during a particularly turbulent and pessimistic period – the aftermath of the destruction of the *Beit Hamikdash* and the

---

60. "וזהו עצמו מה שאיתא בגמרא (במדבר רבה יט, ו) 'וְכָל יְקָר רָאֲתָה עֵינוֹ' (איוב כח, י) דברים שלא נגלו למשה נגלו לרבי עקיבא וחבריו. שרבי עקיבא היה בזמן החורבן, היה מהצורך להאיר אור תורה ביתר שאת. כל שכן דורות אחרונים שאבדנו הכל בעוונותינו הרבים, ואין לנו שיור רק התורה הזאת כמו שכתוב 'לוּלֵי תוֹרָתְךָ שַׁעֲשֻׁעָי אָז אָבַדְתִּי בְעָנְיִי' (תהלים קיט, צב), מהצורך לקיום שלנו שיאירו פירושי התורה... לזאת מאירים לפעמים בדורות אלו דברי תורה בעמקות יותר, כדי שאולי על ידי זה נזכה להטות לבבנו להשם יתברך" (**ליקוטי הרי"ם על תורה ומועדים לרבינו חידושי הרי"ם זי"ע**, אור תורה תש"ע, פרשת חוקת, עמ' שנט).
Note that this resonant statement serves to justify an original explanation of the sin of Moshe. Novel explanations are thus part of the texture of *Torah shebe'al peh*.

tragically abortive uprising of Bar Kokhba – the light of Torah had to shine more radiantly and more powerfully than ever. Precious perspectives on Torah ("And all precious things his eye has seen"), unperceived even by Moshe Rabbeinu, were made visible. Intense preoccupation with and discernible enhancement of Torah was the only effective response to the historical challenge – and this describes R. Akiva and his mission as a *ḥakham hamasorah.* The first Gerer Rebbe adds that this dynamic feature accounts for the fact that sometimes, in these generations, words of Torah are illuminated with greater profundity. This burst of creative energy is a historic-providential need.

The remarkable Rabbeinu Tzadok Hakohen of Lublin – another charter member of the academy of unique *ḥakhmei hamasorah,* who lived in the second half of the nineteenth century – also commented on the dialectic which characterizes the relation between the adversity of dispersion and the glory of creativity:

> The verse "When the ark was to set out" alludes to exile and burdens, for travel is a burden. From this we infer the principle [that the result is] the expanding and building of *Torah shebe'al peh,* the Oral Law. As the Rabbis formulated it: "Sometimes forsaking the study of Torah is [the catalyst for] its reemergence." This was the situation at the time of the Babylonian exile, at which time the Oral Law was established by the *ḥarash,* the craftsmen, and the *masger,* the metalworkers. *Midrash Tanḥuma* interprets the verse in Yeshayahu "Those walking in darkness will then see a great light" as referring to [the experience of] talmudic scholars. Kohelet's words expressed [the idea] "For in much wisdom is much *ka'as,* anger"; this means that as a result of *ka'as* there will be a great increase in *Torah shebe'al peh.*

The verse from Kohelet (1:18), "For in much wisdom is much anger," is interpreted to mean that the increase of anger (*ka'as*), despondency and irritation, brings in its wake an increase in wisdom (*ḥokhmah*), knowledge and understanding of *Torah shebe'al peh.* This paradoxical principle was already discernible during the Babylonian exile, for then the *Torah shebe'al peh* was established. The people walking in darkness saw a great light – profound knowledge of Torah. In a time of exile, of demographic and spiritual dislocation, there is paradoxically a quantum leap in Torah study and creativity. The *ḥakhmei hamasorah* must adopt heroic measures which not only preserve but exponentially increase, deepen, and expand the tradition and reveal its luminousness.[61]

In light of this dialectical principle, we may turn our attention to a remarkable, provocative passage in tractate Gittin:

> What is the meaning of that which is written: "The Lord acted zealously to bring upon us the evil; for the Lord our God is righteous [*tzaddik*]"? How can it be that because the Lord, our God, is righteous, He acted zealously to bring upon us the evil?[62]

This almost sounds like a cruel joke, a perverse, cynical statement made tongue in cheek. If God accelerates the pace so that good events happen quickly, we understand and appreciate that as an expression of His compassion and benevolence. However, zeal with regard to evil – how is that perceived and justified as Divine righteousness? The Gemara clarifies:

> The Holy One, blessed be He, acted benevolently toward the people of Israel by exiling "the exile of Tzidkiyahu" while "the exile of Yekhonyah" still existed [in Babylonia], as it is written with regard to the exile of Yekhonyah: "The thousand craftsmen (*heḥarash*) and the smiths (*hamasger*)."[63]

---

61. וַיְהִי בְּנָסְעַ הָאָרֶץ מרמז על הגלות והטירדא, כי הנסיעה הוא טירדא. חהו דייקא היסוד להרבות ולהבנות על ידי זה בחינת תורה שבעל פה, וכאומרם ז"ל (מנחות כט, ב) "פעמים שביטולה של תורה זהו יסודה". וכמו שהיה מיד בגלות בבל שנתייסדה שם התורה שבעל פה על ידי החרש והמסגר. וכדאיתא בתנחומא (פרשת נח ג) על פסוק (ישעיה ס, א) הָעָם הַהֹלְכִים בַּחֹשֶׁךְ רָאוּ אוֹר גָּדוֹל, אלו בעלי תלמוד. וכמו שנאמר (קהלת א, יח) בְּרֹב חָכְמָה רָב כָּעַס, שעל ידי הרוב כעס בא התרבות החכמה של תורה שבעל פה (**פרי צדיק פרשת** בהעלותך סעיף יד).

62. מאי דכתיב וַיִּשְׁקֹד ה׳ עַל הָרָעָה וַיְבִיאֶהָ עָלֵינוּ כִּי צַדִּיק ה׳ אֱלֹקֵינוּ (דניאל ט, יד) משום דצדיק ה׳ אלקינו וישקוד ה׳ על הרעה ויביאה עלינו? (גיטין פח, א).

63. צדקה עשה הקדוש ברוך הוא עם ישראל שהגלה גלות צדקיהו ועדיין גלות יכניה קיימת דכתיב ביה בגלות יכניה, וְהֶחָרָשׁ וְהַמַּסְגֵּר אֶלֶף (מלכים ב׳ כד, טז) "חרש" שבשעה שפותחין נעשו הכל כחרשין, "מסגר" כיון שסוגרין שוב אינן פותחין, וכמה? אלף (שם).

The answer is based on interpreting *heḥarash vehamasger* in the verse from Melakhim as metaphors for the great *ḥakhmei hamasorah.* The Divine righteousness is manifest in the fact that the last exiles (*galut Tzidkiyahu*) from the Land of Israel arrived while the authoritative, universally respected transmitters and interpreters of Torah were still alive and able to secure the *masorah* among the new exiles. Had more time elapsed between *galut Yekhonyah* and *galut Tzidkiyahu,* the influential transmitters of Torah would no longer have been on the scene; the later exiles would have been doomed to spiritual impoverishment and gradual estrangement from the *masorah* – they would have been caught in the assimilation syndrome.

In American Jewish history, the pattern of immigration was the reverse. *Galut Tzidkiyahu* – large numbers of exiles from Europe – reached the shores of the United States and there was spiritual confusion and desolation. There was little Torah leadership, and the situation of the *masorah* was precarious – it looked as if the ominous possibility of Torah being forgotten (*Torah shetishtakaḥ*) might be realized. People lacked learning and dignity and pride, and the anxiety about the future was deep. In my opinion it is clear that dispassionate and non-partisan chroniclers of American Jewry in the twentieth century (and, by extension, of the fate of traditional Jewry everywhere) will underscore the arrival of the Rov at the end of 1932 as a turning point in the spiritual destiny of American Jewry, as the beginning of the arrival and flourishing of *galut Yekhonyah,* the saving of the battered *galut Tzidkiyahu* as a result of the new vitality, remarkable resilience, and enhanced confidence generated by the *ḥakhmei hamasorah* of *galut Yekhonyah.* The Rov, following in the footsteps of his father Reb Moshe, played a major role in the flourishing of *galut Yekhonyah.* Many other Torah leaders, including the Lubavitcher Rebbe R. Yosef Yitzhak Schneerson and R. Aharon Kotler played important roles as well in the spiritual change, the beginning of Torah renaissance, but the Rov's role was probably the most significant. He emerged as the *ḥakham hamasorah* par excellence.

As was the case with previous *ḥakhmei hamasorah* who appeared at critical moments when people were engulfed by despondency and a sense of futility, the Rov – whose reputation as a youthful prodigy was widespread – emerged on the stage of history and was destined to bring brilliant, beautiful Torah to the twentieth century from his base in Boston and New York. We should not underestimate the impact of one great *ḥakham*. One towering scholar, whose grasp of the *masorah* is majestic and magisterial, whose teaching is original and insightful, whose influence is profound and pervasive, is indeed able to change the entire landscape.[64] The Rov was such a *ḥakham hamasorah*. His decisive contribution was quantitative and qualitative; he disseminated Torah and enhanced *kevod hatorah*. His tireless, vigorous, imaginative teaching, on so many different levels, suffused the *masorah* with new charm and fascination, revealed its profundities, and thereby buoyed the confidence of so many individuals who were demoralized and pessimistic. He energetically and modestly combined the methods of R. Ḥanina and R. Ḥiyya as reported in the Gemara.[65]

The circumstances surrounding the establishment of Maimonides School in Boston and the energies expended subsequently for its maintenance are reminiscent of R. Ḥiyya; the outpouring of *shiurim* and lectures gives substance to the claim of R. Ḥanina. The combination of the

64. עשינו עצמנו בבבל כארץ ישראל, מכי אתא רב לבבל (גיטין ו, א). Note the divergent explanations in Rashi and Tosafot. The Rov wrote as follows about the idea of individual mission and vocation:
"את העובדה שמישהו חי בזמן מסוים, בתקופה מיוחדת ובמקום מוגדר, ולא נולד בתקופה אחרת ובנסיבות אחרות, נוכל להבין אך ורק אם נקבל את עצם הרעיון בדבר שליחותו של האדם. ההשגחה יודעת היכן וכיצד יכול הפרט – היחיד על חסרונותיו וכוחות הנפש האצורים בו, לקיים את שליחותו, באילו נסיבות ותנאים ובאיזו חברה יהא זד בכוחו של האדם למלא את שליחותו... משום כך נברא היחיד בתקופה ובמקום שבהם יוכל לקיים את פעולתו לשם קיום שליחותו" (הרב יוסף דוב הלוי סולוביצ׳יק, **ימי זיכרון**, המחלקה לחינוך ולתרבות תורניים בגולה, 1996, עמ׳ 11).

65. "חנינא בר חמא ישב בראש... והא הוה רבי חייא?... רבי חייא עסוק במצוות הוה... דכי הוו מינצו ר׳ חנינא ור׳ חייא, א"ל ר׳ חנינא לר׳ חייא: בהדי דידי מינצת? דאם חס ושלום נשתכחה תורה מישראל, מהדרנא ליה מפלפולי! א"ל ר׳ חייא: אנא עבדי דלא משתכחה תורה מישראל, דאייתינא כיתנא ושדיינא, ומגדלנא נישבי וצייידנא טביא, ומאכילנא בישרא ליתמי, ואריכנא מגילתא ממשכי דטביא, וסליקנא למתא דלית בה מקרי דרדקי, וכתיבנא חמשא חומשי לחמשא ינוקי, ומתנינא שיתא סידרי לשיתא ינוקי, לכל חד וחד אמרי ליה אתני סידרך לחברך" (כתובות קג, ב). וראו במקבילה, בבא מציעא פה, ב.
[R. Ḥanina claimed that if, God forbid, the Torah would be forgotten, he could restore it through his intellectual acumen and analysis. In response, R. Ḥiyya asserted that he works proactively to ensure that Torah will not be forgotten, by energetically teaching both the Written and Oral Law to as many children as he can; Ketubot 103b.]

methods and characteristics of R. Ḥiyya and R. Ḥanina is truly amazing – a very special fusion of the *vita activa* and *vita contemplativa*: a great teacher and tireless fundraiser for his school, a formulator of enthralling *ḥiddushim* and beautiful categories of thought, a communal rabbi who manifested great *ḥesed* – whether by generous charity, wise counsel, astute guidance, or, indeed, by being available to people who needed to talk with him – while assuming national leadership roles as well.

Indeed, the Rov took his place among the *ḥakhmei hamasorah* and the *ma'atikei hashmu'ah.*

Source Index

במפתח מספרי העמודים של הערכים מופיעים בהדגשה ומספרי ההערות מופיעים בסוגריים. למשל, **40** (18): עמוד 40, הערה 18.

מדרשי הלכה

תלמוד בבלי

תלמוד ירושלמי

שאר מקורות חז״ל

רמב״ם

ראשונים

אחרונים

הרב יצחק טברסקי

Subject Index

The fonts used in this book are from the Arno family

OU PRESS
*Books that educate,
inspire, enrich and
enlighten*

*Maggid Books
The best of contemporary Jewish thought from
Koren Publishers Jerusalem Ltd.*